Half-Truths or Whole Gospel?

*To Jack
with best wishes
Chester Pennington*

Half-Truths
or
Whole Gospel?

Chester A. Pennington

 Abingdon Press—Nashville—New York

HALF-TRUTHS OR WHOLE GOSPEL?

Copyright © 1972 by Abingdon Press

All rights in this book are reserved.
No part of the book may be reproduced in any manner whatsoever without written permission of the publishers except brief quotations embodied in critical articles or reviews. For information address Abingdon Press, Nashville, Tennessee.

ISBN 0-687-16513-X

Library of Congress Catalog Card Number: 74-185546

Scripture quotations unless otherwise noted are from the Revised Standard Version of the Bible, copyrighted 1946 and 1952 by the Division of Christian Education, National Council of Churches, and are used by permission.

Scripture quotations noted NEB are from The New English Bible. © the Delegates of the Oxford University Press and the Syndics of the Cambridge University Press 1961, 1970. Reprinted by permission.

MANUFACTURED BY THE PARTHENON PRESS AT
NASHVILLE, TENNESSEE, UNITED STATES OF AMERICA

To the Hennepin congregation
whose honest intent to be
the people of God in their own place
makes for a life together that is
seldom placid, often excited, always stimulating

Preface

Let's test a thesis: most of the divisions which are tearing at our churches today grow out of different understandings of what is the church's proper business.

I was going to say "inadequate understandings," but that puts us on the defensive. When I hear an adjective like that, I'm inclined to respond, "*My* understanding of the church's function is fine. It's the *other fellow's* understanding that is inadequate." So let's settle for "different." Our thesis then will be that there are several rival understandings of what Christianity is all about, what the church's task is supposed to be; and these differences are causing all sorts of angry tensions in our churches.

Why such differences? Why can't we have more general agreement about the meaning of the Christian gospel and the function of the church? Could it be because we don't pay careful enough attention to the primary sources of this information?

That's a second thesis we might test: Our differences are rooted in insufficient attention to the documents which must be the primary sources for such understanding of Christianity and the church. Obviously, this means the New Testament.

If there is any measure of truth in these theses, what is needed is a careful and honest study of the New Testament. And the way things are today, we had better suggest beginning with the teachings of Jesus himself. Such a suggestion is not likely to be greeted by enthusiastic cheers, either by laity or clergy. There are several causes for skepticism about study—quite apart from the fact that it is hard work.

Some are likely to regard study as a distraction from what we should be busy doing. What is important, they may say, is not what we think or believe, but what we are doing.

Well, I would demur at that, perhaps more than demur. Action is certainly important, but we had better know what we are supposed to be doing and why, out of what motives, and for what purposes.

Moreover, I would claim that being a whole and wholesome person is a desirable end in itself. Activists are inclined to say that "being" is not important, "doing" is all that matters, or at best, "being" is for the sake of "doing." I just don't believe it. It's bad religion and bad psychology.

To be a whole person, with a sense of self-realization and fulfillment, is important in and of itself. That's what we are made for. That's what God wants for us. Then it must be added at once that such a person will be concerned about his relations with and responsibilities to other persons. A whole person will surely know this.

A second hesitancy about a call to study is that

Preface

the search for basic agreements, for "reconciliation," may easily become an attempt to gloss over serious differences, to keep the peace at any price, to avoid rocking the boat. I would hope not. Some differences are important and must be held in tension within the life of the church. But understanding these differences, keeping them in perspective, holding them together, require a recognition of and commitment to some commonly held agreements as well.

Surely there must be some common ground on which Christians stand? Surely there must be some possible agreement as to what we believe and what we think we should be doing in society? Re-searching these grounds and agreements can be fun, may even be surprising, and hopefully will strengthen the whole Christian enterprise.

Contents

I. Half-Truths and a Whole Gospel 13
THE WAY IT IS — BUILDING THE CENTER — "THE GATHERING STORM" — WHAT IS THE BUSINESS OF THE CHURCH? — HOW DO WE DO GOD'S WORK? — THE POLITICAL SITUATION — BEYOND POLITICS

II. To Whom Shall We Go? 28
THE INCIDENT — THE QUESTION TODAY — FOR WHAT? — WHY SHOULD WE? — THIS IS OFFENSIVE — THE CLAIM RENEWED

III. What Must I Do? 46
THE INCIDENT — ANOTHER INCIDENT — THE COMMON MEANING — THAT STRANGE COMMENT — THE QUESTION CHANGES — CAN WE TRUST GOD? — A SUMMING UP

IV. Who Is My Neighbor? 72
THE INCIDENT — ON ASKING QUESTIONS — WHO IS MY NEIGHBOR? — ANOTHER STORY:

SAME POINT — WHAT! MY ENEMY TOO? — WAS JESUS A REVOLUTIONARY? — HOW DO WE LOVE? — THE HEART OF THE MATTER

V. *What Do YOU Say?* 98

THE INCIDENT — THE ATTITUDE OF JESUS — HOW CAN WE BECOME? — THE COUNSELOR — THE COMMUNITY OF LOVE

VI. *What Is Truth?* 118

THE INCIDENT — WILLINGNESS TO FACE IT — TRUTH AS PERSON — TRUTH AS AGONY — TRUTH AS CARING LOVE — TRUTH AS POWER — CONCLUSION

I

Half-Truths and a Whole Gospel

A major threat to the effective life of the churches today is our tendency to get hung up on half-truths. Like every other institution in society, the churches are sharply polarized—fragmented may be a better term. I am convinced that a major factor in our polarization is our inclination to seize a portion of the truth and regard it as the whole truth.

One of my favorite professors used to define heresy as the attempt to make a half-truth do the work of the whole truth. The term heresy is not in good standing nowadays. Even the leaders of Christian thought seem unable to determine what it means. So let's simply say that the churches are being torn apart by a very human tendency: We like to grasp a partial truth (which may be manageable), and champion it as if it were the whole truth (which may indeed be much more difficult to handle).

THE WAY IT IS

Let us take this diagnosis as a clue and see if the circumstances in our churches can be described in such terms.

HALF-TRUTHS OR WHOLE GOSPEL?

In order to do so, we must talk in terms of clergy and laity—I want to confess right away that I don't like the word "clergy." All Christians are called to be "ministers." The laity are just as much ministers of Christ as the "ordained" clergy. It is simply that some have been ordained to a special kind of service. All are equally ministers. However, in our time the differences between clergy and laity have been widened and indeed have become a source of tension in the church. So we have to use the terms in order to describe the situation.

Clergymen are, by definition, the preachers and usually the teachers. Many of them are gravely troubled about the current crises in our society, particularly the political, social, and economic dimensions of these crises. This does not mean that laymen are not concerned, but the clergy have fastened upon these issues as constituting a primary professional interest. Many insist that the church, if it is to be relevant, must propose solutions to these problems. So their preaching and teaching consist mainly of worried descriptions of the situation, and impassioned exhortations to get out there and do something about it.

Many laymen are either bemused or bewildered—or both—by what they hear. They are immersed in these practical affairs every working day of their lives, and they think they have acquired some expertise in these areas. They often think they know more than the clergy about such matters—as indeed they may.

When preachers address themselves to some of these concerns, the laymen are rather sure that—at these points—clergymen really don't know what they are talking about. The clergy return the compliment, which really does not help communications.

Laymen are bewildered when they hear about sudden and frequent changes in theological thinking. Their churches may be served by a preacher who will shift from one position to its opposite without batting an eye. In churches that change preachers with some frequency, one man will stoutly contend for a position quite opposed to the one championed by his predecessor. The popular press sometimes features discussions of these varying fashions.

Hearing all this, many laymen conclude that what a person believes does not really matter. So they settle for their own brand of half-truth. This generally consists of what they learned in Sunday school several decades ago, modified by some ideas they picked up in college or in the press, held in uneasy insecurity by a modest respect for the church.

What really grieves me is that many church members today are living on assorted religious half-truths. Their understanding of Christianity is ill-founded, elementary, unexamined, vague. (For instance, many think that to be Christian means to follow a certain ethical code. And, of course, this is what they have been taught in church!)

True to form, many preachers are simply offering newly styled half-truths. To the extent that these ideas conflict with what laymen have already learned, they are not being accepted by church members. The clergy cannot understand why the laymen will not listen.

One possible explanation is that both are hung up on half-truths.

HALF-TRUTHS OR WHOLE GOSPEL?

BUILDING THE CENTER

If this description is at all accurate, it is required that we recover the whole gospel. That is, we must read deeply and clearly the full message of the New Testament. We must read with equal clarity the full range of human need. Then we must try to interpret and implement the whole gospel as it is addressed to the whole person in his total human situation.

Another way of saying this is that the church, like society, is marked by vigorous extremes. These extremes are clear, self-assured, sharp, exciting. They seem to be where the action is.

The center, by contrast—and by definition—is a moderate position. It appears unexciting, conciliatory, even compromising. In a day of sharp conflict, the center is a difficult position to hold. Yet I deeply believe that the center is where the real strength of the church is. It is where the great insight and power of the gospel are. The center is really the exciting and important place to be.

William Butler Yeats, in an agonized poetic vision, cried out some years ago, "Things fall apart; the centre cannot hold."

The center must hold. It is indeed, the only position which can hold together the aggressive and divisive extremes in the church (or in society, for that matter). The center, by definition, must remain open to right and left, willing to learn from each, trying to reconcile whatever is reconcilable in both.

The effort to recover the wholeness of the gospel will result precisely in a strengthening of the center.

Half-Truths and a Whole Gospel

"THE GATHERING STORM"

Let me illuminate our condition by referring to a recent study entitled *The Gathering Storm in the Churches*. The author, Jeffrey K. Hadden, is a sociologist who has used the disciplines of his science to examine the stresses and strains in the church. He sees a "gathering storm," or widening gap between extremists in the churches.

On one side of the conflict is a "new breed" of clergymen, with a few laymen as allies, who are seeking to lead the church into new styles of active involvement in political and economic and social issues. Lined up against them is a majority of laymen—and, I would guess, of clergymen as well—who deny that this is the way the church should go.

Author Hadden's advice is that the new breed should work carefully and sensitively to bring along with them the laymen who now oppose their leadership. He sees the task as one of education and retraining, so that church members will become engaged in the kind of social action their pastors are advocating.

But what if the laymen and clergy who take a different view of the church remain convinced that their position is right? Is it, after all, a foregone conclusion which side is correct? What if the two camps remain locked in bitter opposition? Is all the "learning" to be done on one side? Is it possible that the new breed may have to listen to their opponents—and maybe even learn from them—as well as *vice versa*?

Interestingly enough, Hadden himself gives his support to the new breed. But then he offers some telling criticisms of their ways of operating, which sound surprisingly like those voiced by their opponents. He flatly says that many of these clergymen are simply incompetent to make judgments about some issues, and inadequately informed in their own field of learning! That is exactly what some of their opponents are saying.

If my thesis is at all correct, both sides are stuck with half-truths, and are unwilling to admit it.

WHAT IS THE BUSINESS OF THE CHURCH?

Much of the current conflict centers in our understanding of the mission of the church. What is the church's proper business anyway? There are two common half-truths at this point.

One position popular among some clergymen is arrived at by posing a question: Does the church exist in order to minister to its members or to minister to the world? This kind of question used to appear frequently in professional journals for the clergy. The possibility that it was a spurious question seldom occurred to anyone. It was always put in such a way that there was only one correct answer. As a consequence, many clergymen are stoutly affirming that the church exists not to serve its members, but to serve the world.

The one-sidedness of this half-truth can be seen by asking another question (a non-spurious one, I hope!). Where are we going to get the Christians who will engage in the church's mission to the world? Christians do not just happen. They have to be generated— regenerated, some would say. Christians are not born. If one may use a scriptural figure of speech, they have

HALF-TRUTHS AND A WHOLE GOSPEL

to be reborn. So the question is Where are we going to get Christians?

The answer seems quite clear. That is what the church is for. The church is a place in which to grow Christians, to generate and nurture them. So it has to be said that the church certainly *does* exist for the sake of its members. It is a generating and nurturing community.

But it must be added in the next breath that the church exists *not only* for its members. The church is not just for the "saved." The church is not intended to be simply a nice group, a genteel club for people who enjoy being together; and to the extent that the church has been content to be this, it deserves all the knocks it is getting.

The church certainly *does* exist for the sake of the world. It is a servant community. It is engaged to do God's work in the world. It is to be a witness to the distinctive truth which is entrusted to it. It is to care about people—all people, but especially those who are being hurt by life, who have no other defense, no other champion. The church is to engage in the work of healing human hurts, building better ways of living together, challenging those who are adding to the hurts, and supporting those who are doing the work of healing.

The church is both a nurturing community and a servant community.

HOW DO WE DO GOD'S WORK?

If we agree that churchmen are to do God's work in the world, we have to ask a further question. *How* do

HALF-TRUTHS OR WHOLE GOSPEL?

we do God's work? At once we are caught up in one of the gravest arguments that divide the churches today.

There are some—mostly clergy, I should say—who assert that the church exists primarily as a social change agent. The first task of the church, they say, is to effect radical social change. And the nature of the changes required is always quite clearly defined.

In reaction to this, many laymen, and a large percentage of clergy, take the opposite extreme. They assert that the church exists in order to "save souls" and should have nothing to do with social issues (or have only indirect involvement).

Both of these are half-truths. Baldly stated, each is really false; held together, they both are true. An understanding of the whole gospel will contain both sides of the truth.

Let me try to stake out a tentative position. The church is not primarily an agent of social change. But it is involved in human concerns that point to the need for social change. Such a claim has to be documented scripturally. That is a task for later inquiry. Right now I would like to support it in terms of human need.

Our deepest human needs are not political, economic, or social. These particular concerns are urgent and agonizing today. So we are properly anxious about them. But they are not the basic human needs. We require some sense of the meaning of our lives, the reality of God, the style of life which is appropriate to our humanity and to our society. The church exists primarily to minister to these profound concerns.

Half-Truths and a Whole Gospel

But it must be added at once that the Christian faith certainly has immediate relevance to social issues. So when some of our laymen say that we ministers ought to "stick to religion," we have to reply that these men are in danger of betraying the gospel. If you really understand what Christianity is about, you know that Christians have to be concerned about the kind of society we are building.

After all, we have it on pretty good authority that we are supposed to love our neighbors. It seems clear today that this means, among other things, working to alleviate poverty, to bring war under some kind of effective control, to cleanse ourselves and our social systems from the racism which haunts us, to save our environment—and the list goes on.

How we should go about accomplishing these purposes arouses some of our sharpest and deepest differences. We shall have to do some of our most careful thinking here. But let me say a little in an introductory manner.

During the second quarter of the twentieth century the leading theologians of Christendom made it quite clear that Christians must be concerned about the structures of society. If we are effectively to love our neighbors, we have to build a society in which everyone gets a real chance to live well. Acts of personal charity, conventional deeds of kindness, are no longer enough. We have to build an economy, a political order, a social structure that will open up opportunity to everyone.

This discovery probably had to wait on the development of democratic forms, in which we all share the responsibility for shaping our society. It probably had to wait also on the rude and shocking crises of the first third of our century, which forced us to ask whether some changes might be necessary.

I believe this is a valid discovery. But the word has not yet got through to everybody. Indeed, many laymen violently reject the word when they hear it. Clergymen also react impatiently, not realizing that this is a relatively recent lesson of Christian inquiry, and, in fact, is still seriously disputed in the church. So the debate goes on. The quiet, steady work of Christian education goes on; so quietly, in fact, that many wonder whether anything is really happening.

The mission of the church, then, is a total mission to the whole range of human need. The need for food and work and education, yes; but humans really do not live by bread alone. We also need beauty and worship, purpose and direction, love and community, personal recognition and adequacy. The church is one of God's instruments for ministering to *all* of these—not just some of them, but all.

THE POLITICAL SITUATION

The conflict in the churches has become seriously political. Strictly speaking, it is not a case of clergy versus laity. As I have indicated, there are clergy and laity on both sides of most issues. What may be said is that the laity is becoming more aware of its political power, and more willing to use it.

Let me try to describe the political situation in the churches. Judge for yourself whether you think it is a fairly accurate description.

HALF-TRUTHS AND A WHOLE GOSPEL

In the local congregation the laymen really determine policy and program. At least, this is the way I understand the local church. It is democratically organized and democratically controlled. The clergy has its professional responsibilities, but basically the members of the church determine policy and develop program.

Once we move beyond the level of the local congregation, however, the church is dominated by the clergy. This is probably inevitable. Clergy are paid by the laity to work full time in the church. Therefore, it is quite understandable that the upper echelons of program- and policy-making will be dominated by clergy.

The clergymen who occupy these positions do what they are supposed to do. They use their power to move the church in the direction they believe it should go. They formulate statements on everything from abortion to war. They vote money to groups and programs they believe in. These clergymen are men of deep conviction. They believe they know what they are doing, and they have both the political power and the political savvy to do what they think is right.

Many laymen, on the other hand, are just as deeply convinced that these are not the directions in which the church should be going. They object to the statements made. They believe many of the policies and programs are both dangerous and destructive; but they feel entirely helpless to influence what is happening.

Recently it was my privilege to participate in an informal conversation between clergymen and laymen. We clergy heard very clearly expressed the utter frustration of these laymen and their sense of hurt and anger at the way church politics works. They feel completely shut out of the decision-making processes that determine certain policies and programs. And they are, in fact, shut out. The clergy dominate this whole procedure.

Personally, I think the laymen are quite right in their uneasiness about the system, but I am not enough of a political strategist to see how it can be corrected. The present "storm" must probably continue, with all the discomforts and hurts which political struggle involves. We who believe in democracy as well as Christianity will believe that a larger good can come out of such honest conflict. That is the way democracy works, in the church as well as out.

However, my primary concern is not with politics, but with what I consider more fundamental and lasting issues. What are we trying to accomplish through these political actions? What are the basic purposes of the church? Such questions as these will still be around long after the specific quarrels of the moment have passed. They must be considered even in the heat of immediate conflict. Indeed, they must give direction and meaning to our present actions.

BEYOND POLITICS

One of these days we will have to move beyond politics, and we should be preparing ourselves for these further exercises even while we are in the midst of political tensions.

Conflict may be as necessary an element in the life of the church as of society. But political tactics in themselves will not resolve the conflict that exists or make the church a strong instrument for doing God's work in the world. The time will come when we will have to go beyond politics, and we should be ready for it when it comes. That means preparing ourselves now.

Not long ago I came to know and admire a clergyman who believes in and practices direct political action. He made the interesting observation that when you engage in direct action you always have a negotiating team ready to go into a particular arena when the time is right. That means you must know what you are fighting for and what you are willing to negotiate, before you even engage in political conflict.

There must be a lesson here for us in the church. Politics, yes. But do we know what we want to negotiate for if the battle comes to a standoff? Are we able to define what we believe the church is, what its business really is, and how we would be willing to go about that business? My guess is that most of us are not ready for this metapolitical effort.

What I covet is something I have not been able to achieve very often: free and honest communication among clergy and laity of all varieties of conviction. This requires a higher level of respect and trust than we now have. It requires a willingness to listen to each other. And the church is not marked by such openness on either side.

We have to find some common ground on which we can meet. Is it too far out to suggest that we might try examining the gospel itself? Can we find a common commitment to and an understanding of the Christian faith that will provide a meeting ground for people of varying political and economic persuasion? Can we develop a sufficiently broad center that will hold together the many extremes that mark our life?

This is possible only if all of us are willing to work at achieving such a common understanding of the gospel. Such a task requires that clergy and laity work together, with a willingness to listen to and learn from each other.

Where might we begin?

Is it possible for us to start by taking a deeper reading of the New Testament? That is what I would propose; but you may ask why. Simply because it is the primary source for Christianity. If we don't engage seriously in the lifelong enterprise of understanding the New Testament, we really will not learn much about our faith and its practice—and this is true whether we are clergy or laity.

Where shall we turn to discover the full gospel?

A decade or so ago, some of us would have proposed a careful study of Paul's writings. But Paul is not particularly popular today. In fact, he never was really big with the laity, especially the women.

However, there always has been, and is today, a high regard for Jesus himself. Men and women and youth of many persuasions agree that Jesus is a key figure in the human story. So I propose that we look at the teachings of Jesus in an attempt to arrive at a better understanding of the gospel.

Just so there will be no misunderstanding, let me add that we should consider not only Jesus' teachings as such, but also his actions, not his words only, but his deeds also. What Jesus was, he said; and what he

HALF-TRUTHS AND A WHOLE GOSPEL

said, he did. So we will want to look at his total ministry, teachings embodied in actions, being enacted in doing.

Obviously there are many ways to approach all of this. Let me suggest one which has proved interesting and profitable to me.

In the course of his ministry Jesus was asked several questions that have a curiously contemporary ring about them. Circumstances have changed, but not the issues themselves. The way in which Jesus responded on these occasions can be very instructive to us in our current inquiries.

You will realize, of course, that our discussion cannot be exhaustive. I will try to be representative, but you should be on the alert for what I may leave out. Omission is a subtle kind of censorship, a hidden selectivity that may deny the most vigorous claims to objectivity. I will try to be fair, in both selection and interpretation. But keep an eye on me. I may leave out some very important words or deeds. And my interpretation is always open to challenge.

These chapters, then, are offered as a kind of "first reader" in the study of the New Testament. It is hoped that there will be a rhythm between study and action, that action will be informed by study, and study will be expressed in action.

A recovery of the wholeness of the gospel should lead to a wholeness of personal living.

II

To Whom Shall We Go?

"Give me a clue." This may be just a line in a game or a casual remark, or it may be the expression of a deep-seated human need.

There is psychological evidence that we human beings require some sense of the meaning of our existence. What is the significance of our being alive? As some thinkers put it, why should we *be* rather than *not-be?* (That is really a mind-bending question when you push it.) Is our existence on this planet of any particular importance to the universe, or is the human race, as some philosophers say, an accidental development that will be wiped out in some future cosmic cataclysm?

We need some dependable clue to the answers to such questions. Somewhere we must discover an index that will tell us where to look for the answers. This need is not just casual or occasional, it is profound and persistent. It is not specialized, that is, only for certain kinds of intellectuals. It is universal. We all have the questions in the back of our minds, and we need some dependable answers.

To Whom Shall We Go?

To whom shall we go?

This question seems simple; but don't be deceived. It really embodies what some thinkers regard as a basic issue of our time: the problem of authority. Nothing is more seriously challenged today than our traditional authorities. What is the authority of the teacher? the parent? The weight convention once gave to these offices is largely dispersed. The real authority seems to inhere in the integrity of the persons involved. Surely we all know that the traditional authority of the church has been diminished. We elders ought to admit that the erosion did not begin with today's youth. Most of us accept the authority of the church only when it happens to agree with our own attitudes. This process has moved even further among today's young adults.

The basic issue is whether we have any dependable authority. Is it possible that we are left to our own devices, and everything is relative?

This first subject may seem somewhat abstract and theoretical to you—especially if you are not accustomed to handling such issues. But these are really quite fundamental matters that we have to straighten out before we can go much further.

What or whom do we take as the dependable authority for what we believe and practice? There are many rival claims, many competing faiths, many attractive teachers. To whom shall we go?

This question was addressed to Jesus in exactly these words. The circumstances were rather special and not repeatable. But the way in which the issue was joined, and the way Jesus responded to it, may be instructive to us.

THE INCIDENT
Many of his disciples, when they heard it [Jesus' discourse on eternal life and his claims about himself], said, "This is a hard saying; who can listen to it?" But Jesus, knowing in himself that his disciples murmured at it, said to them, "Do you take offense at this? Then what if you were to see the Son of man ascending where he was before? It is the spirit that gives life, the flesh is of no avail; the words that I have spoken to you are spirit and life. But there are some of you that do not believe." For Jesus knew from the first who those were that did not believe, and who it was that should betray him. And he said, "This is why I told you that no one can come to me unless it is granted him by the Father."

After this many of his disciples drew back and no longer went about with him. Jesus said to the twelve, "Will you also go away?" Simon Peter answered him, "Lord, to whom shall we go? You have the words of eternal life; and we have believed, and have come to know, that you are the Holy One of God." Jesus answered them, "Did I not choose you, the twelve, and one of you is a devil?" He spoke of Judas the son of Simon Iscariot, for he, one of the twelve, was to betray him.—John 6:60-71

Jesus was in trouble. He was having difficulty communicating. Some of the things he was saying irritated his listeners. They challenged him. The more he tried to address himself to them, the more angry they became.

According to our present style of thinking, we would

To Whom Shall We Go?

say that Jesus himself was to blame. We customarily suppose that lack of communication is the fault of the communicator. We are inclined to believe that if we state something clearly and effectively, the listener will accept it. He may not agree with it, but he will not be angered. If he reacts negatively, we say the fault lies in the form of communication.

The possibility that some aspects of the teachings of Jesus are almost unavoidably offensive hardly occurs to us any more. Yet this seems to be the clear indication of the New Testament. Some teachings are simply hard to take, and for a variety of reasons. So the hearer shares in the responsibility of communication.

Communication is a two-way process. Clarity and directness of expression are surely necessary, but so are honesty and openness in hearing.

In any case, those who were listening to Jesus on this particular occasion responded to his troubling words with some irritation. He seemed to be making claims about himself that they found unacceptable. (John 6:41-42, 52). Finally, even some of those who could be called his disciples found the conversation too difficult to follow. These, though not the intimate Twelve, were people who were sympathetic enough to Jesus to be concerned about what he was saying.

Now, however, he had gone too far. They burst out in annoyance, "This is more than we can stomach! Why listen to such words?" (v. 60 NEB).

Once again Jesus' attempts at explanation fell flat. Some of those who were listening simply gave up. They "drew back and no longer went about with him"

(v. 66). We should be quite clear that these were not avowed opponents of Jesus, or people whom he was directly challenging. They were sympathetic listeners. But now they felt themselves deeply offended at some of the things he was saying; and they could no longer go along with him.

This prompted Jesus to turn to his closest followers and ask, Are you going to leave me too?

Peter replied, on behalf of them all, "Lord, to whom shall we go? You have the words of eternal life." Then he added the reason he was able to say this, "We have believed, and have come to know, that you are the Holy One of God" (vv. 68-69).

You might suppose that this strong answer would encourage Jesus. But he must have been feeling very low, because his response to Peter was this: Yes, I've chosen you—twelve of you—and even one of you will turn out to be a devil (v. 70).

THE QUESTION TODAY

We still ask Peter's question, not with quite the same inflection, but with an even more desperate intent. To whom shall we go for the kind of truth that we most deeply need? Some of our most thoughtful contemporaries are troubled by this question.

A prominent scientist wrote that in the near future we will be forced to make decisions that we used to think only God could make. Who should have children? What combination of qualities shall we build into our babies? Who should be allowed to live and who to die? Who shall manipulate whose minds, and to what purposes? This author admits that in order

To Whom Shall We Go?

to make these decisions we need beliefs and values which the sciences themselves cannot supply. To whom shall we go?

A political scientist confesses that politics cannot provide the values to guide political action or the motivation to impel people to responsible concern. If politics cannot direct or propel itself, where shall we turn for the guidance and motivation we need? To whom shall we go?

A student of culture admits that humanistic culture is not self-sustaining. Civilization is the expression of man's deepest needs and aspirations. And these look surprisingly like religion. Our culture must be grounded in something deeper than itself. What, for instance? To whom shall we go?

Admittedly, not all scholars in our time are either so wise or so humble, but there are enough who are to suggest the reality and the urgency of the question.

Most of us—who may not know one scholar from another—know that we have deep personal needs for which we have no ready resources. Each of us asks, What is the meaning of my life? Since I am alive, what should I aim for? How can I live effectively? How can I relate successfully to other people? And if the sciences really cop out, to whom shall I go?

The Christian answer has always been clear and deceptively simple. We turn to Jesus Christ for the definitive word about reality. He gives us the clue to the meaning of life. He shows us what ultimate reality is like. He enacts for us what it means to be human.

Let me make a distinction here that is rather important. It is the church that customarily makes this claim. And many people are turned off by the church, simply because its institutional life is not altogether admirable. I cannot dispute this. In fact, I would add that the church has not always stated its claim either wisely or well. The institution has often said, Come to us for the truth. We know what is right and good. Leave the thinking to us.

Most of us realize that this is a distortion of the genuine Christian claim. We know that if we were to take the church seriously and let it tell us what to think we all would end up in disaster.

However, let us recognize that the church, when it speaks carefully and truly, gets the message right. Take Jesus Christ seriously as the clue to what is basically true about life. He has the words which define and defend the quality of human existence.

FOR WHAT?

There is a further question we must ask. It does not appear directly in the incident as recounted in the Gospel. But, in our circumstances, we have to ask it.

For what sort of truth do we turn to Christ? This has to be considered very carefully. Some of us have come to believe that we cannot turn to Christ for the last word about everything. Rather we go to him for a special kind of truth.

Let us not be misled by the simplified form of the question itself. We are taking our cues from a particular event in the life of Jesus, a question that was put to him in a particular way. But we must not be deceived by the language.

To Whom Shall We Go?

When I suggest that we "go to Jesus" for certain aspects of the truth, I do not intend to speak in the simplistic language of a previous century or even an earlier generation. I am intending to make a serious theological statement. We turn to the whole fact of Jesus Christ, his life and ministry, the scriptural interpretation of him, and the tradition of Christian experience of him. Here we find a dependable insight into what is really true about ourselves and our world.

This does not mean that we can simply assert "the Bible says—" as our final authority. The Bible is of crucial importance, to be sure, but its importance is precisely its witness to Jesus Christ. And that brings us back to the present question. For what kind of truth do we turn to Christ?

Let me state it first negatively.

We do not turn to Christ for scientific truth. He was not a scientist, and the Bible is not a textbook of science. The perennial problems of the alleged conflict between science and religion would be eased if only we would admit that science is not religion and religion is not science.

We do not look to the teachings of Jesus for instruction in politics or economics. We have no evidence that he ever imagined a democratic society or a highly industrialized economy. He was not a sociologist. He was not a psychologist, in today's professional sense of the word. He was a man of extraordinary insight, to say the least, but he was not a clinician or an analyst.

You may protest, But wasn't he the Son of God? He was indeed. But this is a far more complex affirmation than you may guess. For instance, we have to take the

HALF-TRUTHS OR WHOLE GOSPEL?

doctrine of the Incarnation quite seriously. If we believe that Jesus was God incarnate, we believe that he was a genuine human being too. In him God was undergoing a fully human experience. This means that, as a man, Jesus was limited to the scientific and sociological understandings of the first century. He was not an expert in anything and everything, and we should not expect to turn to him for all sorts of truths about every subject under the sun.

We turn to Christ for the particular sort of truth to which he was profoundly dedicated. And what is that?

It is my honest judgment that Jesus chose to address himself to a precise and carefully drawn area of human concern. We shall have occasion to test this conviction, as we actually examine his teachings. I believe he spoke to the fundamental human issues: the meaning of our existence, the reality of God, how you and I may achieve fulfillment, how we may relate to one another successfully.

I take this to be our contemporary equivalent of what Peter meant when he said to Jesus, "You have the words of eternal life" (v. 68). This is what we turn to Christ for: the words of eternal life.

Once again, don't be betrayed by the simplified form of expression. We must take Peter's words to refer to the purpose of our human life, the truth about human destiny and how it may be achieved. What does God want us to be? What are the divine purposes for our human existence? These are the questions to which Jesus offers dependable guidance. He gives us the clue we need; better yet, he *is* the clue we need. Note the word "clue." I have chosen it carefully and deliberately.

To Whom Shall We Go?

It indicates my belief that Jesus Christ does not give ready-made answers to all the questions we can think up. He gives us dependable clues to the solution of our most urgent questions.

We will turn to other branches of human learning for answers to many important issues. We will turn to Jesus Christ for the answers to our deeper inquiries into meaning, purpose, motivation, fulfillment, destiny. He has these "words of eternal life."

WHY SHOULD WE?

Now we are driven to a basic question: What is the ground of Jesus' authority? Why should we turn to him for this—or any—kind of definitive truth?

When we stop and think about it, this is an extraordinary claim. Jesus was a simple, relatively untrained man. He lived, in an obscure corner of the Roman Empire two thousand years ago, a comparatively primitive style of life. He is about as remote from our contemporary technological civilization as anyone you can imagine.

Why on earth should we say that we should turn to this sort of man for any kind of word that is relevant to our time? We don't do it in science, in business, in politics, only occasionally in philosophy—indeed, not in any significant area of human life. Why should we make such a claim in religion?

As far as I can discover, there is really only one answer to this question. It is basically what Peter said in explanation of his own confidence in Christ: "We have believed, and have come to know, that you are the Holy One of God" (v. 69).

HALF-TRUTHS OR WHOLE GOSPEL?

Translated into contemporary language, this means: In Jesus Christ, God is communicating himself with a freedom and a fullness which he has not achieved anywhere else in the whole history of man. This is the distinctive and central claim of the Christian faith.

Incidentally, I am impressed with the fact that in the New Testament there is no single way of expressing this extraordinary assertion. It appears almost as if the several writers of these documents were struggling with words, trying to say what may be inexpressible, and using everything in their vocabulary that seemed appropriate.

If this observation is true, it is instructive for us. The central claim has to be made: Jesus Christ is "the Holy One of God." But our use of this incident must not cause us to oversimplify the affirmation. There is no single way of stating it, and we dare not insist that it be expressed in any particular words. There must be freedom to declare this remarkable faith in every way possible. There must also be concern that the declaration not be diluted or distorted but remain authentic and genuine.

Interestingly enough, this affirmation seems to have been challenged from the first day it was made. In the Gospel records there are accounts of disputes concerning the authority of Christ—and sometimes for reasons which sound remarkably contemporary.

In the seventh chapter of John's Gospel the discussion continues. We note with much interest that even Jesus' brothers failed to believe in him. He couldn't even win his own family. (See v. 5.)

The opponents of Jesus were the intellectual and

To Whom Shall We Go?

religious leaders of his people. They challenged his authority by questioning his background. How can his teachings be sound, they asked, when he has never been properly educated (v. 15)? Then they uttered what they thought would be the crushing indictment: How many educated persons, how many people in positions of leadership are taking him seriously (v. 48)? The implied judgment is that people who are really well informed will not pay attention to such an untrained man. Only the simpleminded and uneducated will be taken in by him. (I remember hearing something like that in college, backed by serious sociological statistics.)

Doesn't that sound remarkably up-to-date? Jesus is too far removed from us to be relevant, some say. How, they ask, can his simple teaching have any real significance for our technological, sophisticated society?

Jesus' defense of himself is the best answer we can give: What I am saying is not my own idea. It is what God is giving me to say. I have no authority of my own, only what God gives me. If you have the courage to take me seriously, you will soon find out whether I am speaking on my own or whether my teaching is from God (vv. 16-17).

It may be worth noting that Jesus did not always reply in so direct a way to those who questioned his authority. Perhaps circumstances determined the nature of his response.

During the last week of his ministry, Jesus had come into direct conflict with his opponents. His actions were radical: a demonstration on entering the city, a confrontation in the Temple. His teachings were sharpening the issues still further.

His opponents challenged him: "By what authority are you doing these things?"

Jesus countered with another question: Where do you think John the Baptist got his authority?

His challengers realized that they would be caught, no matter how they answered that one. So they evaded the issue: "We don't know."

Jesus replied, You dodged, and you know it. So I am not going to declare myself to you either. You are not ready to take me seriously. (Cf. Mark 11:27-33, and parallels.)

However, there never was any doubt in the author's mind as to the real authority of Christ. Mark announced his work as "the gospel of Jesus Christ, the Son of God" (1:1). And this faith is implicit in the entire gospel, as indeed it is in the other three as well.

Actually, in one form or another, this is really what we must affirm today concerning Jesus Christ. He is a very special person. In fact, he is one of a kind. No one quite like him had ever happened before, and has not since. There have been other seers and prophets and mystics and teachers, and we can learn from them all. But what is valid in these others can be known and evaluated and tested by reference to the one person who is like—yet strangely unlike—them all. Because in him God succeeded in uttering himself with a clarity achieved nowhere else among men. In him God was free to act with a fullness never possible in the life of any other man anywhere.

How would you say it? Words are inadequate, but

we must be sure this is what we say. We turn to Jesus Christ because God is uniquely present in him.

This is what many of Jesus' own contemporaries could not stomach. The claim was never made blatantly or brazenly. But when it subtly began to clarify itself, there were many who could not take it. They turned away. This was too much. They were offended.

THIS IS OFFENSIVE

Let's be honest. Such a claim is still offensive. This is the basic reason why Christianity—real Christianity—will never win a popularity contest. This is why it will never become a mass movement in Western civilization. It is simply offensive to too many people.

I see no way to avoid the offense. If we eliminate the claim, we betray the gospel. If we are faithful to the gospel, we must affirm the unique authority of Christ (not the church, mind you, or any particular dogma, not the Bible, but Jesus Christ himself). And such an affirmation is offensive in two troubling ways.

To affirm the authority of Jesus Christ is an offense to our confidence in our own intellect. We say that in Christ, God is disclosing to us a truth which we cannot discover for ourselves. Moreover, we are saying that God is able to make this disclosure through Jesus Christ in a manner which he never quite managed anywhere else in history.

This offends our intellectual pride. We prefer to believe that we can figure things out for ourselves. We want to think that we can discover, by our own rational powers, whatever truths we need. Moreover, there are many wise men, we add, whose teachings commend themselves to our innate recognition of what is wise and good.

But the Christian faith says, No, you are really not up to this. Ultimate truth is beyond your grasp. If you are to know God, he must disclose himself to you. And you must be willing to receive his disclosure, to let yourself be grasped by it. You can take it or leave it, but you can't make it up yourself.

Such a claim is offensive in another dimension. It offends our moral pride. Because the assertion is not only that God discloses himself to us, but that in this real man he discloses us to ourselves.

In Jesus Christ we see what we are intended to be. Apparently only God can live a fully human life. And once we see the divine intention bodied forth, we recognize that we aren't quite up to that either.

Through Christ we see that we suffer from a deep-rooted illness which we ourselves cannot heal. What God does in Christ is necessary to the healing of this illness. There is something seriously wrong with us human beings. We seem to spoil everything we do. We cannot get along with one another without anger and violence. We are thoroughly mixed up and quite incapable of straightening ourselves out. So God comes to us in Jesus Christ and does what is necessary to make possible our healing.

Such a claim offends our moral pride. We prefer to think that we can work things out by ourselves. Give us enough education, enough sensitivity, enough time, and, we say, we'll solve our own problems. We believe we have the capacity to make our human life what it ought to be. So when the Christian faith asserts otherwise—that we will bungle every well-intentioned effort—we are annoyed. We won't listen.

Actually, it was Paul who experienced the shock of this offense most clearly. It is entirely understandable that it should happen this way. Jesus could not say everything about himself. Indeed, maybe it wasn't all that clear to him. In any case, he could hardly interpret the full significance of his death and resurrection. This had to be left to his interpreters.

Paul, therefore, preached about the cross and its meaning for our human condition, and he ran headlong into trouble. He quickly learned that such ideas are unwelcome to the proud self-confidence of men. We hate to admit that we need anything, even God. And to be told that we will die from our own unadmitted illness, unless we accept the healing which God offers, well, we'd almost rather die first. We are turned off by such talk.

The claim will always be offensive. Let us not pretend that we can ever make Christianity an attractive, genial religion that will charm everybody into good-natured acceptance. Christianity is really too tough-minded for that. Too honest. Too realistic.

Let us seize the offense, and experience its healing.

THE CLAIM RENEWED

The primary address of the Christian affirmation is to our will. It quickens the imagination, stirs the feelings, commands serious thought, but primarily and most profoundly it asks for our willingness to decide in favor of the person who is represented.

Jesus himself said: "If any man's will is to do his [God's] will, he shall know whether the teaching is from God or whether I am speaking on my own authority" (John 7:16).

There it is. If we want to know the validity of the Christian faith, we have to take it seriously enough to try it. We must test it. Turn it over. See how it works. But we must do this with utter seriousness, and it will prove itself to us by the new quality of our lives.

So the long discussion about authority becomes at last a very personal address. Will you take seriously, for yourself, this claim of Christ? Will you turn to him for the definitive words by which you will live?

You may reply that you are a church member, and you have been most of your life, or that you are a clergyman, ordained to the service of Christ and his church. And you may ask why such a question should be put to you.

My answer would have to be that our status as church members or clergymen does not necessarily mean that we have answered this question satisfactorily. My ordination is no guarantee that I am an authentic Christian, and neither is your church membership.

We have to face this issue candidly and honestly. Do we really take seriously the authority of Jesus Christ? We have ranged far and wide in our consideration of what his authority means. And we must do this because of the broad range of human concerns. But the issue has special pertinence to the divisions which plague us within the churches which bear the name of Christ.

To Whom Shall We Go?

What is the real authority for the positions you are taking and defending so stoutly? Are you willing to expose yourself and your convictions to the light of Jesus' teachings? Are you clear where his teachings are relevant and where you may be bending them to fit other persuasions which you cherish?

Are you willing to let yourself be examined as a person? Where is your primary loyalty? What are your real values? Is it possible that the position you champion is a reflection of your own pride or self-interest? Or that the opposition you express toward another position is a reflection of a hidden hostility? Or can we say that beneath the causes which we champion is a fundamental loyalty to Jesus Christ, that deeper than the conflicts which divide us is our common commitment to him?

The Christian claim is direct and clear. Jesus Christ is "the Holy One of God," and therefore ought to be the leader of our lives. The words he speaks about our existence and our destiny are divinely authenticated, and therefore ought to mark out the purposes and directions for our living. His loving acts are charged with divine power, so that our own frustrated capacity for love may be released. His call to obedience and service claims our response, so that together we become his "body," the instrument for doing his work in the world.

III

What Must I Do?

One of the most persistent questions asked by church people is this: What must I do? The implication is that Christianity must include certain requirements. If I am to consider being a Christian, what am I expected to do?

Invariably the accent is on the word *do*. The question usually means, "Give me a specific and practical answer, something I can get my teeth into."

Frankly, I'm not at all convinced that people really want such specific instructions. Suppose, for instance, that I did come up with a few suggestions. Let's say I propose ten rules for you to follow—there is some precedent for that number. The idea would be that if you did these ten things, you could consider yourself a Christian.

I'll bet I know the first thing you would do. You would edit the list. You would single out certain rules which seem to be "practical"—that is, within reach of your ability and agreeable to your present thinking. You would find ways to soft-pedal one or two others that seem a little too demanding. You would manage

What Must I Do?

to forget at least one. (How many of the original ten can you name?)

So the question really cannot be answered in terms of rules. Somehow we have to go deeper than your interest in practical suggestions. We might ask why you choose some rules and minimize or actually eliminate others. Why do you keep asking for specific things to do, when you find it difficult to observe the rules you already have?

The question itself is real enough. What may be inappropriate is our expectation. That is, we may be looking for the wrong kind of answer. We have been trained to expect a set of ethical instructions. But if we ask the question openly, we may be directed toward something quite different. At least, it's a possibility. So let us not approach the issue with the assumption that we know what the answer is going to be. And let us stay with Jesus' response long enough to get the full impact and range of what he had to say.

This specific inquiry was addressed to Jesus on at least two occasions of which we have a record. It seems reasonable that Jesus' answer to such a direct question should be quite basic in our understanding of what a Christian is supposed to do.

THE INCIDENT

And as he was setting out on his journey, a man ran up and knelt before him, and asked him, "Good Teacher, what must I do to inherit eternal life?" And Jesus said to him, "Why do you call me good? No one is good but God alone. You know the commandments: 'Do not kill, Do not commit adultery, Do not steal, Do not bear false witness, Do

HALF-TRUTHS OR WHOLE GOSPEL?

not defraud, Honor your father and mother.' " And he said to him, "Teacher, all these I have observed from my youth." And Jesus looking upon him loved him, and said to him, "You lack one thing; go, sell what you have, and give to the poor, and you will have treasure in heaven; and come, follow me." At that saying his countenance fell, and he went away sorrowful; for he had great possessions.

And Jesus looked around and said to his disciples, "How hard it will be for those who have riches to enter the kingdom of God!" And the disciples were amazed at his words. But Jesus said to them again, "Children, how hard it is to enter the kingdom of God! It is easier for a camel to go through the eye of a needle than for a rich man to enter the kingdom of God." And they were exceedingly astonished, and said to him, "Then who can be saved?" Jesus looked at them and said, "With men it is impossible, but not with God; for all things are possible with God."—Mark 10:17-27. (See also Matthew 19:16-26; Luke 18:18-27.)

The first occasion on which this question was addressed to Jesus is recorded in all three of the Synoptic Gospels. You will recall that Matthew, Mark, and Luke are called the Synoptic Gospels because they can be looked at together. They parallel one another to a very great degree. There are distinctive differences, too, which must be noted, so it makes for a fascinating study.

If we put together the varying Gospel accounts, the story is something like this.

Jesus was about to leave town. As he and his disciples started out into the street, an attractive young man came hurrying up to them. He knelt before Jesus, expressing at once his respect and his sincerity. (As

What Must I Do?

you know, Jesus was not always approached in this manner, which makes this particular incident all the more striking.)

Good Teacher, the young man said directly, what must I do to achieve what true religion offers?

I used to think that Jesus' reply to the young man was rather curt: "Why do you call me good" (v. 18)? But listening to the conversation a little more imaginatively, I have come to the conclusion that Jesus was good-natured and relaxed in his response. I think he must have grinned a little and replied pleasantly:

Be careful with your adjectives, young man. I appreciate the compliment, but there is really only one being who deserves to be called good, and that is God. And, as you very well know, we ought to look at the laws he has given us to find an answer to your question. You know the rules.

Jesus cited a few typical laws, to illustrate what popular religion expects of its followers.

The young man answered, Teacher—since you prefer no adjective—I have kept these commandments ever since I first learned them as a boy.

Something in his manner really got through to Jesus. Jesus liked what he saw in the young man, but he certainly took a strange way of saying so.

There is only one thing lacking in you, Jesus said. Get rid of your possessions. Just sell them and give the money away to people who need it; and then come with me.

Now what on earth possessed Jesus to say a thing like that? Something in the young man's bearing or the cut of his clothes may have indicated that he put a pretty high value on his social standing, or he may have had a reputation in the community for holding a rather high opinion of himself. Whatever the reason, Jesus certainly chose a strange way to show that he really liked the man.

In any case, it was just too much. The young man turned away regretfully. He simply could not meet such an uncompromising demand.

Now let us pause for a minute. Let's not rush on too quickly. What should we make of this?

Our immediate reaction to the conversation is to pass it off by saying that, of course, Jesus does not make such a demand of everybody. This was a special instance, we say, and we should not universalize it. It would be quite impractical to imagine that Jesus would ask such a thing of everybody (we hope).

True enough. But to say this too quickly or too easily is to avoid the force of what Jesus is doing. We ought to pause over this long enough to let it sink in.

Jesus is confronting this attractive young man with a stark, uncompromising demand. He might not put it to us in quite the same manner. But we all have an uneasy suspicion that Jesus confronts us with an uncomfortable equivalent, and we have every sympathy with the young man as he backs off.

Jesus watched the man leave, and his own shoulders must have sagged as if in sympathy with the retreating figure. Jesus sighed and commented to his disciples: It certainly is difficult for people with money to get into the kingdom of God.

The disciples were surprised at his remark. They placed much value on money as the rest of us. In fact,

What Must I Do?

they could have put the young man's resources to good use in the life of their own circle. (They must have wondered why Jesus didn't propose that.) They couldn't understand why Jesus would say that people who have money had difficulty making it into the Kingdom.

So Jesus repeated himself more graphically: It is easier for a camel to get through the eye of a needle than for a rich man to squeeze into the Kingdom.

The disciples were really confused by this time. So they asked, Then who can manage it?

Jesus replied with a strange word: "With men it is impossible, but not with God; for all things are possible with God" (v. 27).

End of story!

How is that for a practical answer to a practical question? You can't do it, but God can.

What are you going to do with this? Maybe it would be easier to conclude the lesson somewhere else, but where? True enough, the account goes on to discuss specific issues which the disciples raised. But that simply gets us off the track.

Here is the conclusion to the incident. The disciples asked who will succeed in getting into the Kingdom; and Jesus answered, You can't do it, but God can.

Let's hold the conclusion right there while we look at another incident in which the same basic question was asked.

ANOTHER INCIDENT

On another occasion Jesus was asked what we should do in order to achieve the values promised by religion.

HALF-TRUTHS OR WHOLE GOSPEL?

As we compare the parallel accounts in the Synoptic Gospels, some interesting differences appear. We do not want to be distracted by details, but we must know why we choose to consider the passage we do examine.

Luke's record states the question in the same terms that we have already considered: "Teacher, what shall I do to inherit eternal life" (Luke 10:25)? But there are so many distinctive marks of this account and we have to consider them in another connection, that we had better look at the other Gospels.

Matthew and Mark phrase the question differently, but it is the same issue. What are the most important rules for us to observe? What are we expected to do? Matthew's account is simple and direct, so let's use that one.

> *But when the Pharisees heard that he had silenced the Sadducees, they came together. And one of them, a lawyer, asked him a question, to test him. "Teacher, which is the great commandment in the law?" And he said to him, "You shall love the Lord your God with all your heart, and with all your soul, and with all your mind. This is the great and first commandment. And a second is like it, You shall love your neighbor as yourself. On these two commandments depend all the law and the prophets."—Matthew 22:34-40. (See also Mark 12:28-34; Luke 10:25-28.)*

The inquirer was a well-educated, highly trained man who was broadly informed about matters of religion and ethics. He asked Jesus what is the most important rule for us to follow.

Jesus answered with his famous summary of the

What Must I Do?

law. There are two great commandments to observe: You must love God with all the powers of your being; and you must be as concerned about your neighbor's good as you are about your own.

When you and I read this passage, or hear it referred to, we almost always jump quickly to the second of these two commandments. It is more immediate and practical, we think. Obviously we do have to give it careful attention, but I believe it is entirely unfair to skip over the first commandment too quickly. It is, after all, the first. The second has force precisely because it is related to the first.

I propose that in order to be fair to Jesus' answer we must allow ourselves to be confronted by the total demand of that first commandment. When asked what we must do, Jesus replied, You must love God with all the powers of your being.

What does that mean? In this instance, love cannot mean a feeling. We are not commanded to feel about God in a certain way. Besides, we don't order our feelings around. So the word has to mean an attitude, a way of action.

This command must mean that our concern to do God's will should be the determining factor in our life. These words must reflect the first commandment as stated in the Decalogue: "Thou shalt have no other gods before me" (Exodus 20:3). Or as Jesus stated it on another occasion, "Seek first his kingdom" (Matthew 6:33). That is, let the primary aim of your life be to do what God asks you to do. Direct your life so as to fulfill God's purpose for you.

Quite apart from the difficulty of determining just

what it is that God expects of us, I have recently experienced a deeper discomfort at this command. The force of that word *all* began to get through to me.

We are commanded to address ourselves to doing the will of God with *all the powers of our being*. We are to concentrate *all* our powers and direct *all* our efforts to the achievement of his purposes for us.

THE COMMON MEANING

As we sense ourselves confronted by this total demand, we can pause to ask whether there is any common element between Jesus' reply to the rich young ruler and his answer to the talented, educated leader. I think there is.

In each instance we are challenged by what one New Testament scholar has called Jesus' "demand for radical obedience." That is, what Jesus is asking for is not simply obedience to a command; what he wants is an obedience which is a response of our whole being to his total claim on us. So when the rich young man asked what he should do, Jesus bluntly replied, Get rid of everything that stands between you and total obedience to God. Just get rid of it. And come with me.

Similarly, the command to love God is a demand for total response. Love God with all the powers at your disposal. It is not just the rich young man who was asked to do the impossible. It is every one of us who allows himself or herself to be confronted honestly with this first commandment.

Oh, I know what usually happens. The words are so familiar that we hardly hear them. Moreover, we

What Must I Do?

protect ourselves against the full demand by automatically reducing its content. God cannot mean this literally, we say. We have to give our powers to other legitimate demands on us. Every one of us is therefore hung up on his or her second-rate interests and commitments.

When I let that word *all* really get through to me, I begin to make excuses. "I'm sorry, Jesus, but I really can't manage this. I have a wife and family to consider, and a job. I want my children to have an education. There are a few niceties of life I'd like to enjoy. And then there's retirement. Can't we make some kind of adjustment in this demand?"

But I hear no adjustment coming from the lips of Jesus. He looks at me—kindly, I think, but rather firmly too—and he says, "I'm sorry. Don't talk to me about all those worldly interests. They are really not my concern. You asked me what you should do, and I'm telling you. You must love God with all the powers of your being."

Is that all? You mean all?

That's what I said.

Man, what am I going to do?

THAT STRANGE COMMENT

Allow the demand to stand just as it is, stark and uncompromising. Then we may be able to sense the significance of the puzzling word of Jesus that concluded the conversation in the first incident. Remember what he said, "With men it is impossible, but not with God; for all things are possible with God" (Mark 10:27).

It is as if Jesus was saying, A man asked me what he should do. When I told him, he could not do it. Then you, my disciples, asked me, If this man can't make it, who can? My answer is that it is quite impossible with you as humans. It is possible only from the divine side. What you cannot do, God can make possible for you.

Admittedly, this is a strange word. What on earth can it mean?

I take this to be Jesus' initial and tentative affirmation of what we have come to know, under the tutelage of Paul, as the grace of God. What God demands, he gives. He does not reduce the demand. He does not accommodate it to our inadequacies. He wants our total obedience, yielded from the core of our being. To settle for less, for instance, a handful of rules, would spoil our life. We would soon lose our humanity. Rather than allowing this, God makes it possible for us to be what he demands.

The validity of this interpretation can be indicated, I think, from the records themselves. For instance, Matthew follows his account of the first event with the puzzling parable of the laborers who worked different numbers of hours but received the same pay (Matthew 20:1-15). Luke precedes his account of the same incident with the story of the Pharisee and the publican (Luke 18:9-14). We shall turn to these stories later. They seem to reinforce my present interpretation.

What is perhaps even more significant is that Paul made the same kind of statement just as succinctly as Jesus did, and in a strikingly parallel manner.

What Must I Do?

Jesus said, What is impossible with man is possible with God.

Paul said, What the Law could not do, God has done (Romans 8:3). Then Paul went on to add what Jesus himself really could not have said.

This is what Jesus Christ is all about. The significance of his life and ministry, his death and resurrection, is that God is affirming a radical reversal of the common understanding of religion. What God requires is not that we perform certain duties in order to win his favor. What God requires is that we receive the love and personal power that he manifests in Jesus Christ.

What God demands, he gives. He enables us to become what he wants us to do.

THE QUESTION CHANGES

The radical reversal of religion is the shift of emphasis from God's demand to his gift, from our attention to duty to our acceptance of grace. This is the most profound and original impact of the ministry of Jesus.

When we sense the full force of this radical change the question we ask undergoes a corresponding change. It is no longer What shall I do. The question becomes Whom shall I trust. And Jesus addressed himself to this also.

Every once in a while, Jesus was approached by a person who was obviously proud of his status and achievements, and who was clearly relying upon these accomplishments to win the favor of God. Consistently, Jesus tried to point out to such persons that they were putting their trust in the wrong place. They should trust not their own faithfulness, but the faithfulness of God.

I do not know whether Luke had a particular quickness to pick up such implications, or whether those who reported these events to him were sensitive to the circumstances, but the insight comes through most often in Luke's record.

The lawyer who was questioning Jesus about what he should do was not satisfied with the first answer and pressed his question further. Apparently he did this because he wanted "to justify himself" (Luke 10:29). That is, he was trying to build up his own achievements as a basis for acceptance with God.

Similarly, Jesus addressed a telling parable to "some who trusted in themselves that they were righteous and despised others" (Luke 18:9).

A scorching criticism of some skeptical Pharisees was: "You are those who justify yourselves before men, but God knows your hearts" (Luke 16:15).

In every instance, Jesus is trying to destroy self-confidence and replace it with trust in the goodness and power of God.

I have to grin every time I remember some conversations I have had about a comment recorded in Matthew. Jesus was talking with some good religious citizens, and he said, "The tax collectors and harlots go into the kingdom of God before you" (Matthew 21:31*b*).

The troubled ladies who read this have said to me, "If this is true, why should we bother to be decent, law-abiding citizens, faithful to our husbands? If this

What Must I Do?

kind of person is going to enter the Kingdom before our kind, what's the point?"

The answer is to read further. Why does Jesus say that these disreputable characters will "go into the Kingdom"? Because, when John the Baptist preached to them, they believed, and the so-called good people never did take him seriously. (Cf. v. 32.) The definitive difference was faith and unfaith.

Jesus did not indicate whether the shady businessmen and harlots ever stopped their respective trades. We may hope, from the example of others, that they did. Zacchaeus certainly cleaned up his enterprise; and Mary Magdalene changed her way of life. What Jesus said in this comment is that what makes the difference in the quality of a person's life and destiny is his or her response of faith.

Oddly enough, in some of these accounts an interesting implication creeps in. We seldom hear reference to it today. The implication is that not many people are going to be able to accept this radical reversal.

Several times Jesus was questioned whether what he was saying implied that not many would be saved. Every time he replied in the affirmative: Yes, it is unfortunately true that only a few will make it.

> *Enter by the narrow gate; for the gate is wide and the way is easy, that leads to destruction, and those who enter by it are many. For the gate is narrow and the way is hard, that leads to life, and those who find it are few.—Matthew 7:13-14*

> *And some one said to him, "Lord, will those who are saved be few?" And he said to them,*

Half-Truths or Whole Gospel?

"Strive to enter by the narrow door; for many, I tell you, will seek to enter and will not be able."
—Luke 13:23-24.

You might think that what Jesus was saying would make it easier to follow him. What, no rules? But we sense that his insight is far more radical and more searching than any series of rules could possibly be.

Jesus does not impose specific requirements. He demands our total commitment to God; and he makes the strange assertion that God is willing to give us what he demands of us. That is, God will elicit, by his love, the response which his goodness requires. Jesus asks that we put our trust in God. What counts, he says, is not the excellence of our dutiful performance, but the integrity of our response to God's love.

As I reflect on these different comments of Jesus, I invariably think of his conversation with Nicodemus (John 3:1-15). There are important differences between this man and ourselves. But the likenesses are significant enough for us to take notice.

Nicodemus is sometimes criticized for coming to Jesus at night, as if he might have been a little uneasy. Personally, I think he came in the evening for a very good reason. It was the only time he could find Jesus alone long enough for a decent conversation. They could talk at leisure, and they probably did.

At some point in the conversation, Jesus chose to become somewhat more direct. Nicodemus, he said, what you need is a brand new beginning, one that only God can make possible for you (3:3).

When Nicodemus had difficulty grasping this (Why

What Must I Do?

is it always so hard for us to understand what grace means?), Jesus reaffirmed his meaning: This is something that only God can do. You need to receive a new life that he can give you. (Cf. vv. 6-8.)

It remained for Paul to make it clear that this is what Jesus is all about. Christ not only redefines what religion ought to be (trust before duty), but he embodies God's gift of new life.

CAN WE TRUST GOD?

This remarkable reversal does not stand by itself. There is, in fact, a substantial body of teaching in which it must be placed, and by which it is supported. Jesus reinterprets the meaning of religion on the basis of his understanding of both God and man. Christ's assertion of what God expects us to do is based on his insight into what God does for us.

Jesus not only urges us to put our trust in God. He affirms that God is trustworthy. Jesus gives a radical interpretation of the response God wants from us. He offers an equally radical understanding of the divine effort to evoke that response. What God wants us to do, Jesus says, is grounded in what he is willing to do for us. God does not give commands, he gives himself. The divine self-giving is for the purpose of eliciting our giving of ourselves to him in obedience and love.

Here we turn to those teachings of Jesus which the Gospel writers had placed in rather close relationship to the main incident discussed in this chapter. The arrangement may be accidental, and I would not want to hang too much importance on mere proximity. How-

Half-Truths or Whole Gospel?

ever, it is perfectly clear that these teachings do strengthen and round out the insight which I have called a radical reversal of conventional religion. If this reversal were stated only in an occasional comment, we might well wonder whether it is especially important. But when we bring together the substantial teachings which relate to the insight itself, we know that we are reckoning with a central and commanding element in the meaning of Christ's message.

So Matthew records a very strange story which Jesus told.

> *For the kingdom of heaven is like a householder who went out early in the morning to hire laborers for his vineyard. After agreeing with the laborers for a denarius a day, he sent them into his vineyard. And going out about the third hour he saw others standing idle in the market place; and to them he said, "You go into the vineyard too, and whatever is right I will give you." So they went. Going out again about the sixth hour and the ninth hour, he did the same. And about the eleventh hour he went out and found others standing; and he said to them, "Why do you stand here idle all day?" They said to him, "Because no one has hired us." He said to them, "You go into the vineyard too." And when evening came, the owner of the vineyard said to his steward, "Call the laborers and pay them their wages, beginning with the last, up to the first." And when those hired about the eleventh hour came, each of them received a denarius. Now when the first came, they thought they would receive more; but each of them also received a denarius. And on receiving it they grumbled at the householder, saying, "These last worked only one hour, and you have made them equal to us who have*

What Must I Do?

borne the burden of the day and the scorching heat." But he replied to one of them, "Friend, I am doing you no wrong; did you not agree with me for a denarius? Take what belongs to you, and go; I choose to give to this last as I give to you. Am I not allowed to do what I choose with what belongs to me? Or do you begrudge my generosity?" So the last will be first, and the first last.—Matthew 20:1-16

Frankly, this story has always bothered me. It runs against my sense of fair play. Any practical person must wonder what on earth Jesus means.

A landowner hired laborers to work for the day at an agreed wage. At later hours he brought in other men with no specific arrangement as to salary. In fact, it was almost the end of the working day when he hired the last group.

Then when the time came to pay them, the landowner gave every man the same amount, regardless of how long or short a period he had worked. Obviously, and understandably, the men who had worked all day were upset about this. To them it was totally unfair.

The employer's only response to their complaints was that he had paid the first group what they had agreed upon as a fair wage. If he chose to give the same pay to the other men, that was his privilege. "Or," he added with a sly dig, "do you begrudge my generosity" (v. 15)? Well, of course we do!

It is only recently that, thanks to a shrewd New Testament scholar, I have been led to see what Jesus may be saying here. It is almost as hard to swallow as the story itself.

Half-Truths or Whole Gospel?

God does not reward us on the cold balance of our merits. He freely offers us his love and forgiveness. His acceptance of us is not something we can earn by performing certain duties. He freely extends his acceptance to us, to be received gracefully. It is difficult for us to understand his "generosity," because that is not the way we operate. But God does not treat us the way we expect him to.

That's what Jesus is all about.

In much the same way, and yet very differently, Luke underscores the identical insight by recording a striking parable.

> *He also told this parable to some who trusted in themselves that they were righteous and despised others: "Two men went up into the temple to pray, one a Pharisee and the other a tax collector. The Pharisee stood and prayed thus with himself, 'God, I thank thee that I am not like other men, extortioners, unjust, adulterers, or even like this tax collector. I fast twice a week, I give tithes of all that I get.' But the tax collector, standing far off, would not even lift up his eyes to heaven, but beat his breast, saying, 'God, be merciful to me a sinner!' I tell you, this man went down to his house justified rather than the other; for every one who exalts himself will be humbled, but he who humbles himself will be exalted."—Luke 18:9-14*

The real shocker here is the first half of that fourteenth verse. Don't be distracted by the second half. The punch line is the first part: "This man [the obvious sinner] went down to his house justified rather than the other [the equally obvious 'good' man]."

What Must I Do?

I would bet that not a dozen members in an average congregation today believe this. Jesus must be kidding.

Two men went to the Temple to pray. One was a religious, civic-minded man, entirely confident that he was doing the things God expected him to do. He was properly thankful for the blessings he enjoyed and quite sure that God was pleased with the way things were going.

The other man was a person caught up in the compromises of his employment. He was sure he had no moral status at all. So the only thing he could say was, "God, be merciful to me a sinner!"

The incredible conclusion Jesus draws at the end of this contrast is that the latter man went home justified, accepted by God, rather than the former. This was a complete reversal of all the regular religious ideas that Jesus' contemporaries accepted, and on which we ourselves have been brought up. If we were not so familiar with the story, we would realize how radical and devastating the conclusion really is.

Jesus is saying that what God requires of us is not the careful, calculating performance of such duties as we think proper. What God asks is that we entrust ourselves to his mercy. We are not to put our confidence in our own achievements as the means of winning the rewards of religion. We are to trust the faithfulness and goodness of God, and commit our lives to his purposes.

That's what Jesus is all about.

While we are thinking about this striking aspect

of the teachings of Jesus, we really ought to turn briefly to one of the most remarkable chapters in the Gospels.

In the fifteenth chapter of his Gospel, Luke brings together three parables that make the same radical reinterpretation of the meaning of religion. Interestingly enough, it was the same sort of self-trust, which becomes self-righteousness, which evoked these most dramatic statements concerning the trustworthiness of the God in whom we are to place our entire confidence. (Cf. vv. 1-2.)

If you had a hundred sheep, Jesus said, and realized that one was missing, what would you do? You would see that the flock was in a safe place, and then go out to look for the sheep that was lost. When you found it, you would bring it home, call together your friends and neighbors, and celebrate. What was lost had been sought for and found. (Cf. vv. 3-7.)

Or, he continued, if a woman had misplaced part of her life savings, you know what she would do. She would turn the house upside down until she found it. Then she would call in her neighbors to share the good news with them. What had been lost was now found. (Cf. vv. 8-10.)

In both instances the point is precisely the same. This is the way God is. He does not wait for us to find him. He looks for us in our confusion and loneliness and rebellion. He seeks to evoke our response of acceptance, trust.

The same affirmation is made even more dramatically in the familiar story of the prodigal son. The attractive but willful young man leaves home and wastes his brilliant gifts in the squalid indulgences of the underworld. But his father's love is unchanging. Indeed, the father runs out to meet the boy who had "come to himself" and was turning toward home. Again the refrain is the same: Let us celebrate because the one whom I feared dead is alive; the one who was lost is found. (Cf. vv. 11-24.)

Quite remarkably, the story is not yet over. An older brother had remained faithful to his father and spent his life in respectful obedience. We all are familiar with his angry response to the news that his younger brother had returned, and that his father had called for a celebration. What we seldom note is that the father addresses himself to the proud anger of his older son in just the same way that he had met the humbled, penitent boy. The father goes out to the ill-tempered, self-righteous son and urges him to come in where he belongs (v. 28*b*). We do not really know whether this "lost" son is "found." But we do know that the father goes out to find him. (Cf. vv. 25-32).

That's what Jesus is all about.

It is important to note that Jesus not only talked like this about God, but he also acted like this in his ministry. He not only said that God seeks the lost, he himself went out to look for them. Jesus is the embodiment of the seeking love of God.

Amusingly enough—yet understandably—this was the occasion for one of the most frequent criticisms of Jesus. He really was not very careful about the company he kept. He went to anyone who needed him. He responded gladly to anyone who was open to his approach. This took him into the company of many morally disreputable people. When criticized, Jesus simply replied, That's the way God is.

One day Jesus was passing through Jericho. Zacchaeus, the district director of internal revenue, lived there, and made quite a fuss about trying to see Jesus as he was walking through the city. In fact, he caught the attention of Jesus so effectively that Jesus actually invited himself to Zacchaeus' home, much to the shocked surprise of the decent citizens of the city.

Jesus' only defense was, "The Son of man came to seek and to save the lost" (Luke 19:10).

That's the way God is, actually seeking out those who are lost and bewildered and frightened, so that he may give them direction and confidence and hope.

That's what Jesus Christ is all about.

A SUMMING UP

What does all this add up to?

Well, in the first place, we have brought together a substantial body of the teachings of Jesus. These are not just occasional sayings, here and there, like a series of proof texts. Taken together, they represent a major element in Christ's message. Moreover, these teachings articulate a radical element in the ministry of Jesus that is often neglected. We are dealing here with a radical reinterpretation of the central significance of religion.

When we are asked what Jesus taught, we usually think of the Golden Rule or similar moral exhortations. But the thrust of what we have studied in this chapter

What Must I Do?

is to drive beneath such moral teachings and get at our basic motivation. Jesus simply turned the conventional notion of religion upside down—or is it right side up? The essence of true religion, Jesus said, is not grim performance of duty but glad acceptance of grace.

How did we come to this conclusion?

When Jesus was asked what we should do to fulfill our religious obligations, he confronted his questioners with an impossible demand. We are inclined to temper this demand to our own tastes. But I find no evidence that Jesus ever did this, or encouraged anyone else to do so.

When challenged about the reasonableness of such confrontation, Jesus seemed to respond by saying, Why don't you just admit that it's impossible, and look more deeply into what God has to offer you.

When pressed further, Jesus indicated that it is unwise to try to build up our own accomplishments as a way of approaching God. What God wants is that we simply trust his love.

Then in the most original and creative achievement of his whole ministry, Jesus portrayed, in both word and deed, the character of God as one who loves his human creatures, loves them so much as to endow them with an undeserved grace, to seek them in their loneliness, and to try to bring them home where they belong.

Here we have Jesus' own statement of what Paul would later expound as the doctrine of "justification by grace through faith." We usually think of this doctrine as an invention of Paul. It was not at all. It was the central insight of Jesus himself. It was, in-

HALF-TRUTHS OR WHOLE GOSPEL?

deed, the primary intent of his ministry. It is in Paul only because it was in Jesus.

Now let me hasten to add that we are not finished yet. There is much more to be studied. We must not jump to conclusions at this present point. But there's no mistaking the radical character of what we have discussed thus far. It should help us establish some priorities in our understanding of ourselves and of the church's task.

Oddly enough, it is very difficult for us to hold fast to this insight—or maybe not so odd. This aspect of Christ's teaching relates rather directly to the offense of the gospel which we mentioned previously.

We find it annoying to be told that we cannot be self-reliant, that we have to depend on somebody else —even God—for our well-being. We'd rather do it ourselves. But Jesus gives us no basis for this.

Jesus affirms clearly that God does not simply give us a body of rules to obey. Rather God says, You really can't make it; but let me show you what I can give you. God does not wait until we tidy up before he lets us approach him. He actually seeks us in our untidy mess, and tries to draw us into his fulfilling care.

A frequent temptation is to reduce this radical teaching of Jesus to one of the two half-truths we noted in the first chapter, and to emphasize what is popularly called "personal salvation." This may sound like what Jesus is saying, but often such an interpretation is tied in with a fixed vocabulary and with strict styles of personal morality. If we are not careful, the gospel is reduced to a new legalism. Jesus said more than this,

What Must I Do?

and we can't stop here. What we should be careful to do, however, is to stay here long enough to sense the full impact of his message.

Coming through with striking clarity and power in these teachings of Jesus is the radical insight that the heart of Christian faith and experience is the acknowledgment of our own ineptness and the acceptance of the surprising offer of God. He wants to give us the new life which we anxiously try to generate for ourselves.

You may object that this is all very theoretical and impractical. I should reply that, at this point, I don't notice that Jesus was particularly concerned about being "practical." He seems to have been more interested in getting at the root of the human situation. He finds the basic human need right at the very heart of every person, an inner reality too deep to be measured by ordinary methods, namely, our central relation with God.

But that's not all. Don't stop here. There's more to come.

IV

Who Is My Neighbor?

Our next inquiry leads us into the consideration of our social responsibility as followers of Christ. The preceding question was intensely personal: Are you willing to be open to God at the private decision-making center of your self? The present question is inescapably social: Are you willing to be open to your fellow human beings in honest and active concern?

The occasion which evokes this issue is recorded in Luke's Gospel. We recognize it at once as comparable—apparently and initially, at least—to an incident mentioned in Mark and Matthew. I say "initially" because Luke's story, after beginning in the same way, takes off in another direction. I say "apparently" because Luke's account has so many significant differences as to suggest that it may be a record of another occasion altogether.

These distinctive marks may simply be due to the differing recollections of Luke's informant, as over against Mark's source and Matthew's (who probably relied on Mark anyway). But there is also the possibility that the same question was put to Jesus on differ-

Who Is My Neighbor?

ent occasions, in different ways, and therefore evoked different responses.

My own personal hunch—strictly unofficial—is that Luke has recorded a conversation different from that recounted in the other Gospels. There is certainly no reason why Jesus could not have been asked the same question by various people. And Luke's story is so distinctive that I prefer to imagine it to be an entirely separate occasion. But it doesn't matter; the record is here, and it is most interesting.

THE INCIDENT

And behold, a lawyer stood up to put him to the test, saying, "Teacher, what shall I do to inherit eternal life?" He said to him, "What is written in the law? How do you read?" And he answered, "You shall love the Lord your God with all your heart, and with all your soul, and with all your strength, and with all your mind; and your neighbor as yourself." And he said to him, "You have answered right; do this, and you will live."

But he, desiring to justify himself, said to Jesus, "And who is my neighbor?" Jesus replied, "A man was going from Jerusalem to Jericho, and he fell among robbers, who stripped him and beat him, and departed, leaving him half dead. Now by chance a priest was going down that road; and when he saw him he passed by on the other side. So likewise a Levite, when he came to the place and saw him, passed by on the other side. But a Samaritan, as he journeyed, came to where he was; and when he saw him, he had compassion, and went to him and bound up his wounds, pouring on oil and wine; then he set him on his own beast and brought him to an inn, and took care of him. And

Half-Truths or Whole Gospel?

the next day he took out two denarii and gave them to the innkeeper, saying, 'Take care of him; and whatever more you spend, I will repay you when I come back.' Which of these three, do you think, proved neighbor to the man who fell among the robbers?" He said, "The one who showed mercy on him." And Jesus said to him, "Go and do likewise."—Luke 10:25-37. (See also Mark 12:28-34; Matthew 22:34-40.)

Jesus' questioner was a man of culture and social position. Hebrew religion was closely involved in the regulation of daily life and in the social practices of the nation. So when the man is identified as a "lawyer," he should not be thought of in terms of our present-day legal profession. Rather he was a man thoroughly trained in the traditions and customs of his national culture, which was profoundly and inescapably religious.

The initial question is the one we have already discussed. What shall I do to gain the benefits of true religion? But this time Jesus did not answer. Instead, he turned the question back to the man himself.

Jesus said, You know the answer as well as I do. You are a scholar. What do you read?

And the man answered his own question. He stated the twofold summary of the law: Love God and love your neighbor.

Jesus replied, You are exactly right. That is all you have to do. Follow through, and you will enjoy a full life.

Now we have to stop and note a striking fact about this conversation. The famous twofold summary of the law has popularly been attributed to Jesus, but

Who Is My Neighbor?

in Luke's record it is stated not by Jesus but by one of his Jewish contemporaries. This is very significant. It implies that the summary is not necessarily original with Jesus, but was taught by some of his contemporary rabbis. The commentaries I have consulted indicate that this can be documented out of the literature of that century.

Here's the point. The twofold summary of the law may not be particularly distinctive of Jesus' own teaching. He may simply be reflecting the best of some of his contemporaries. He is not saying anything here that other rabbis of the period could not have said.

Let that sink in.

I find it ironic, but not exactly amusing, that the popular teaching of the church has made so much of this particular item. I would guess that most church members—and most preachers—if asked to summarize the teaching of Jesus, would reply with the Golden Rule and this double law.

But neither of these is uniquely Christian; both are simply summaries of Jewish teaching. To regard these as the epitome of Christ's ministry is to reduce him to an Old Testament prophet, or less, a first-century rabbi.

The linking of these statements is not as original as the insight we expounded in the previous chapter, and certainly not as radical. There Jesus was saying something which apparently none of his predecessors or contemporaries could ever bring himself to say. Here he is simply reflecting the insights of other wise teachers.

Moreover—and I find this even sadder—the summary of the law is usually interpreted in a moralistic manner. The net result is to reduce Christ's teaching to a new form of legalism. And it was precisely legalism which he was trying to overcome and replace with new understanding.

ON ASKING QUESTIONS

An interesting editorial insight in this record is worth noticing. We have commented before that Luke or his source seems to be sensitive to the little nuances of these conversations. Someone has been aware of the slightest hint of self-righteousness or insincerity on the part of an inquirer, and has inserted it in the record.

So in Luke's account there is the suggestion that the man who questioned Jesus was not altogether serious in making his inquiry. In the first place, it is said that he was trying to "test" Jesus (v. 25), perhaps even to trap him. He was not necessarily being malicious, but at least his motive was not the pure desire to learn.

Moreover, he knew the answer to the question before he asked it. When Jesus turned the issue back to the man, the response was quick and certain. The man already knew the answer. He didn't have to ask. He was playing games.

He should have quit while he was ahead. But no, he wasn't content with the initial dialogue. He was anxious to "justify himself" (v. 29). That is, he wanted to put himself in the best possible light. He wanted to come out of the exchange looking good.

This leads me to reflect that we can use questions as a diversion from the real issue. We often know the

Who Is My Neighbor?

answers, but we keep on raising questions. We simply try to avoid the implications of what we already know. We pretend lack of certainty, when it is really courage we lack. Our questions are not doubts but dodges.

Let me be clear. I have every respect for honest inquiry. There is no question a Christian should hesitate to raise, whether he can find an answer or not. There is no particular virtue in pretending to know all the answers. There is great virtue in pressing the right questions. James Thurber tells a delightful fable, the moral of which is: "It is better to ask the right questions, than to know all the answers." A profoundly true observation.

The fact remains that sometimes we keep asking questions in order to evade what we already know. The trouble with certain kinds of truths is, they make demands on us. So we think that if we can challenge the truth, we can reduce the demand.

Jesus does not play that kind of game, not with this man, and not with us. He keeps turning such questions right back to us.

In fact, have you ever noticed that when Jesus finally did address himself to the man's further inquiry, he did not answer that question either? This famous story does not tell us directly who our neighbor is. It puts the pressure on us to act like neighbors to our fellow humans.

So the man asked, "Who is my neighbor?" (v. 29).

Jesus answered with a story, and countered with another question: "Which of these three, do you think, proved neighbor to the man who fell among the robbers?" (v. 36).

In other words, the real question is not Who is your neighbor. The real question is To whom are you willing to act like a neighbor, to whom are you willing to respond with genuine caring.

It is as if he says to us: I'm not going to play games with you. You know where the real issues are. Are you willing to be the kind of person you know full well I want you to be? That's the only issue that really matters. We can look for answers to other interesting questions—after we've settled that one.

WHO IS MY NEIGHBOR?

However, the question is a real one. The story Jesus told answers it indirectly but unmistakably. I warn you, in advance, you will not be comforted by his reply.

The second great commandment, Jesus had agreed, is that you are to be as concerned for the good of your neighbor as you are for your own good. You are to seek his well-being just as earnestly as you seek your own.

Who, then, is my neighbor? To whom do I owe this kind of concerned action?

In response to this, Jesus told a story which has become almost too familiar to us. A man was beaten and robbed and left alongside the road. Two religious leaders came by. They saw him, and went on without troubling themselves about his condition. Then a member of a minority group came along, saw that the man needed help, and responded with much more consideration than could have been expected.

At the conclusion of the story Jesus asked this ques-

Who Is My Neighbor?

tion, Who turned out to be a real neighbor to the man who was in trouble?

And the answer was easy, "The one who showed mercy on him" (v. 37).

Jesus shrugged and said, The implication is obvious. You should do the same.

The indirect answer to the man's question, then, is something like this. Anyone who has a need to which I have the capacity to respond has a claim upon me. Everyman is my neighbor. Or what is perhaps more significant, I am called upon to act as neighbor to every man. Those who are hurt and limited and endangered by circumstances of our common life have a special claim upon our concern. We are to love them as we love ourselves. That is, we are to seek their good with the same honest concern as we pursue our own good.

It may be in order to comment here that these human needs are not always of the physical and measurable kind of which we are so much aware in our time. We all know the desperate needs of many of our fellow human beings who are poor, deprived, who really do not have a chance at some of the benefits of our society. We ought also to realize that there are other kinds of needs: for friendship, for understanding, for cultural opportunity and values, for instruction and good taste. These needs may not always be so obvious or so desperate as the former, but they are just as human and just as real.

So here we are confronted again with one of those total demands which seem to admit of no compromise or exception. We are commanded to be as concerned about the well-being of our fellow humans as we are about our own. (By the way, who can manage to do this? Any quick volunteers?)

ANOTHER STORY: SAME POINT

Jesus told another parable which makes the same uncomfortable point. The story is quite different from any other he ever told (scholars have noted this difference). But the implication it carries is the same as that of the classic story we have just read. Incidentally, this parable has become very popular among some of our teachers and preachers in recent years. Frankly, I think it is frequently misused, misinterpreted. It is made to say more than it really says. The intent of the parable, seen in the context of Jesus' total message, is not so simple as sometimes imagined; but it is part of the record, and we must pay attention to it.

> *When the Son of man comes in his glory, and all the angels with him, then he will sit on his glorious throne. Before him will be gathered all the nations, and he will separate them one from another as a shepherd separates the sheep from the goats, and he will place the sheep at his right hand, but the goats at the left. Then the King will say to those at his right hand, "Come, O blessed of my Father, inherit the kingdom prepared for you from the foundation of the world; for I was hungry and you gave me food, I was thirsty and you gave me drink, I was a stranger and you welcomed me, I was naked and you clothed me, I was sick and you visited me, I was in prison and you came to me." Then the righteous will answer him, "Lord, when did we see thee hungry and feed thee, or thirsty and give thee drink? And when did we see thee a*

Who Is My Neighbor?

stranger and welcome thee, or naked and clothe thee? And when did we see thee sick or in prison and visit thee?" And the King will answer them, "Truly, I say to you, as you did it to one of the least of these my brethren, you did it to me." Then he will say to those at his left hand, "Depart from me, you cursed, into the eternal fire prepared for the devil and his angels; for I was hungry and you gave me no food, I was thirsty and you gave me no drink, I was a stranger and you did not welcome me, naked and you did not clothe me, sick and in prison and you did not visit me." Then they also will answer, "Lord, when did we see thee hungry or thirsty or a stranger or naked or sick or in prison, and did not minister to thee?" Then he will answer them, "Truly, I say to you, as you did it not to one of the least of these, you did it not to me." And they will go away into eternal punishment, but the righteous into eternal life.—Matthew 25:31-46

The story portrays the final judgment of the world. The exact identity of the judge is never clearly established: Son of man, King. He represents, we may suppose, God as judge.

The King calls all the people before him and renders final judgment. What is the basis of his discrimination? Human destiny is determined by the way people have responded to their fellowmen who were in need.

Why should their destiny be so determined? Because these needy persons are persons for whom God cares. God identifies with these human creatures who are in desperate circumstances. So the King says to those before him, I was in need and you ministered to me.

The people respond with surprise, When did we minister to you in any way?

And the King replies, "As you did it to one of the least of these my brethren, you did it to me" (v. 40). I care so deeply about these, my human creatures, that I call them my brothers. I identify with them in their need. So that as you minister to them, you are ministering to me.

The same inescapable message: human beings who are hurt and deprived by life are persons for whom God cares. We are to care about them enough to serve them as if we were serving God, as indeed we are. The way to love God is to love your neighbor.

WHAT! MY ENEMY TOO?

As if this weren't bad enough, we all know that Jesus pushed the commandment even further. We remember, uneasily, that Jesus went so far as to suggest that we should love our enemies. Unrealistic and impractical as it seems, that is exactly what he did.

He said something like this: The old rule was that you should love your neighbor and it doesn't much matter how you treat your enemy. Be as cool or as cruel as occasion demands. But I say to you that you should love your enemy also. I want you to be concerned about the well-being of your enemy. He is your neighbor too.

> *You have heard that it was said, "You shall love your neighbor and hate your enemy." But I say to you, Love your enemies and pray for those who persecute you, so that you may be sons of your Father who is in heaven; for he makes his sun rise*

Who Is My Neighbor?

on the evil and on the good, and sends rain on the just and on the unjust. For if you love those who love you, what reward have you? Do not even the tax collectors do the same? And if you salute only your brethren, what more are you doing than others? Do not even the Gentiles do the same? You, therefore, must be perfect, as your heavenly Father is perfect.—Matthew 5:43-48

Notice that Jesus did not say that we won't have any enemies. Let's not make believe. We will have lots of rivals, opponents. Sometimes the stakes are very high. What Jesus said is that we are to contrive somehow, no matter how bitter the competition, to keep the best interests of our enemy in mind. We are to seek his good.

When we start thinking about candidates for this category, we think most easily of those whom our nation calls enemies: citizens of countries with whom we are in conflict; adherents of rival ideologies.

But what about those whom we regard as "enemies" in a somewhat subtler sense. Business and political rivals. How about the angry, the violent? Those who advocate the overthrow of the system we believe in? Those who are willing to destroy values we cherish?

We may think of these as enemies. Actually, some of them may not be, but let's not minimize the sharpness of Christ's word. We are to "love" them. That's what Jesus said. There are those dear hearts and gentle people whom it is easy to like (though this doesn't mean we actively "love" them). But we are commanded to be equally concerned about the troublesome and unattractive rebels who are so hard to understand. They are not just our "enemies," they are our neighbors. We are to care for them.

In our dismay we are likely to ask, Why on earth should we love our enemies? We'd be well rid of them. This is really too much to ask. Why not forget it?

Jesus' reply is what we have seen it to be on other occasions: That's the way God is. He happens to love them, your enemies, just as he loves you. And if you're going to be his child, you'd better act like a member of the family (vv. 45, 48).

Now let me confess that I don't know what to do with this kind of talk any more than you do. The fact that I'm a clergyman makes such teachings no easier to understand, and certainly no easier to practice. So if you ask me what this is all about, I have to join you and ask the same question.

But I have to report what Jesus said, as directly and honestly as I know how. No compromising. No adjustments. No pretending. Just plain reporting. And here it is: Love your enemies.

Help!

WAS JESUS A REVOLUTIONARY?

Of course Jesus was a revolutionary. I have tried to indicate just how radical he really was. That is, he was determined to get at the root of our human condition. He insisted on stating God's intention with sharp and uncompromising honesty, no matter how it shook conventional ideas. His real radicalism was, of course, religious.

But was he a revolutionary in the current political sense of the word? Was he—would he be—a champion

Who Is My Neighbor?

of radical social change? Before you answer too quickly, let's look at the record.

It may come as a surprise to some of you that some Christian spokesmen interpret Jesus as a revolutionary in the tradition of Marx and Mao. They see him as bitterly opposed to a social system of cruelty and exploitation. They portray him as ready to take violent action to destroy such a system in order to make way for a better one.

The basis for this interpretation is not his teachings themselves. As you can guess, it would be difficult to pinpoint many sayings which support the use of violence. The understanding of Jesus as revolutionary is based on his actions, particularly his action in cleansing the Temple. In fact, this is just about the only deed which can be cited (Mark 11:15-18 and parallels).

The Temple, it is said, was the symbol of all that was bad in the Establishment, an alliance of religion and politics that exploited the poor to the advantage of the rich and powerful. Jesus' charging into the Temple, smashing the tables and driving out the exploiters, it is contended, was his violent attempt to bring down the corrupt system so that a new one could be set up.

What is the evidence that leads to this conclusion?

First, there was a revolutionary political party in Jesus' day. Its members were advocates of armed rebellion against the Roman Empire. They were called Zealots. They championed the cause of Jewish liberation from Rome by violent destruction of the governing power.

In fact, there was at least one member, or former member, of the Zealot party among Jesus' disciples.

HALF-TRUTHS OR WHOLE GOSPEL?

Simon is called "the Zealot" (Luke 6:15; Acts 1:13. Mark 3:18 uses a different word, usually regarded as the Aramaic term for Zealot.). However, it is not at all clear whether Simon remained an active member of the party after becoming a follower of Jesus. It all depends on how you interpret the next question.

Is it possible that Jesus himself was a Zealot? Some New Testament scholars defend the thesis that he was at least a sympathizer. A few go so far as to say that Jesus advocated the use of violence, as seen in his attack on the Temple.

The way they arrive at this conclusion, however, is just a little circuitous. First they assume that Mark covered up the violent side of Jesus' ministry. The reason he did so, they suppose, was to shield the new Christian movement from the jealous power of Rome. So they conclude that he simply edited out some of Jesus' rougher sayings and tidied up some of the evidence.

Well, when you assume that Mark has tried to cover up something, all you have to do is to read into the record whatever you assume he covered up. And, presto, you have Jesus the Zealot. (I don't want to belittle serious scholarship, but this looks as if you first put a rabbit in the hat, then look impressed when you pull it out!)

Let me say that I am quite confident that this interpretation will not prove out. I am not enough of a scholar to handle the subject thoroughly myself. However, I do try to keep abreast of current scholarship; and the men to whom I look for guidance are agreed that this theory simply cannot stand rigorous, careful examination.

A friend of mine, who is very sensitive to social issues, simply says, "Every time I try to get Jesus to join one of the groups I happen to believe in, he just walks away." That is, Jesus refuses to be identified with any particular political group.

What happens, I think, is this. People approach the New Testament with their own particular persuasion. They read into the teachings and ministry of Jesus the enthusiasm they are championing. This is not hard to do really, but it is not recommended procedure.

So the Marxist interprets Jesus as a social radical. The American capitalist portrays Jesus as the wise businessman or the clever public relations expert. Either way, Jesus is betrayed.

What the revolutionaries manage to overlook, or to explain away, is the far more impressive body of teaching in which Jesus simply refuses to support violence. He just won't have anything to do with the usual methods of coercion. When you come right down to it, it is pretty difficult to imagine someone who said "love your enemies" inflicting violence on his own opponents.

Equally impressive is Jesus' reluctance to have people call him Messiah. It was a popular political title, with all the overtones of violence associated with a political liberator. Jesus cautioned his disciples about their use of the term, and he seems consistently to have refused to use it for himself. He preferred to speak of himself as Son of man, or Servant, terms which did not carry political implications.

Half-Truths or Whole Gospel?

What positive conclusions may we draw from this?

It was the tradition of the Hebrew prophets not only to speak, but also to demonstrate against the religious-social system when they found it corrupt and exploitive. There is something of this same prophetic character in the ministry of Jesus.

The entry into Jerusalem, for instance, was surely a public demonstration (Mark 11:1-11, and parallels). Some developments may have been spontaneous and unexpected. But there is evidence in the story that Jesus had planned it ahead of time, that there had been prearranged signals, as in asking for and releasing the colt, for example.

But what was Jesus demonstrating? Scholars are not altogether clear as to the meaning of the event. At least Jesus is declaring himself leader of his people; but he enters the capital city in humility and with peaceful intent.

Similarly the cleansing of the Temple was a kind of "direct action." Jesus knew human nature well enough to know that those who hold power are not going to give it up unless they are forced to do so. So he struck a dramatic blow against the religious-social system which was willing to use religion as an instrument to depress the poor and powerless. His aim, I would guess, was not so much to destroy as to cleanse.

It ought to be clear that Jesus, as a man of peace rather than violence, threw all his weight against any acts of injustice and exploitation. His sympathies went out quickly to the poor and dispossessed. And they turned to him, drawn by his compassion. He was scathing in his indictment of those who abused their re-

Who Is My Neighbor?

ligious and political status. And they turned away from him, offended by his integrity.

This should be kept in mind when we try to fathom his puzzling statement about Caesar and God: Render unto each what belongs to him (Mark 12:13-17). But that's just the problem. What does belong to each? We often quote this saying, as if it offered great help. But, actually, Jesus never told us which is which. We still have to figure that out for ourselves.

Let's try a suggestion or two, gleaned from this chapter's inquiry into our relations with our neighbors. God wills the good of every man. We may call some people "enemies," but God loves them too. Caesar—the state—really exists in order to serve God's purposes, that is, to minister to the good of men. But Caesar inevitably takes sides. It is the national government which calls some people "enemies."

To the extent that Caesar actually contributes to and makes possible the larger good of men, he deserves our allegiance. But when he serves some men at the expense of others, and when, to top it off, he calls himself god, he does not deserve our service. We must challenge him, perhaps deliberately disobey him, precisely in the name of our primary allegiance to God.

HOW DO WE LOVE?

How do we express our love for our neighbor? In the rough-and-tumble of real life, how do we implement our concern for the well-being of our fellow citizens?

This is one of the gravest issues in the churches today—and indeed in society at large. It is, in fact, one of the problems that are tearing us apart. The intense and sometimes violent differences in approach to this question are largely responsible for the political conflicts that are dividing our churches into opposing camps.

It probably has to be this way. Love has to be politicized. And political action is usually pretty rough, even when carried on in the name of love.

Let me try to draw a few conclusions from our study of the ministry of Jesus. Remember now that I have no intention of presenting a program of action. My concern is, first, to understand what Jesus had to say about these issues, and second, to see what guidance we can gain from him.

Frankly, I think we receive very little practical instruction in politics from the teachings of Jesus. His command is unmistakably clear: you must really care about what happens to your fellow human beings. The motivation is profound: this is the way God is and wants you to be. The practical implementation is—dare I say—nonexistent.

The fact is, as far as I can see, Jesus gives us little or no specific instruction in the ways and means of loving our neighbor in a complex, industrialized, technological, democratic society.

There is no possible misunderstanding of the imperative. We are under orders to seek honestly the best good of our fellow citizens (citizens of the world, that is). The practical question is how we are to do this. And, at this point, when I turn to the New Testament, I draw a blank.

There are two reasons for this. First of all, in a somewhat philosophical vein, love does not provide

Who Is My Neighbor?

its own methodology. Our concern for our neighbor has to be expressed in economic, political, social terms. Love, in itself, does not provide instruction in politics and economics. Love is an attitude, a determination to act in a particular manner. That determination must be translated into political and economic and sociological policies and programs.

These policies and programs have to be tested, not simply by the ideal of love, but by the realities and theories of politics, economics, and sociology. At these points, men and women of apparently equal concern and wisdom disagree profoundly and widely, often bitterly. In these issues, love cannot help us, except to enable us to keep our heads and hold on to our solid motives. These issues are examined in terms of the disciplines and practices involved, whether political, economic, or social.

There is a second reason why I don't find the New Testament especially helpful in these matters. In my judgment Jesus never addressed himself to such problems. Jesus was not a political scientist; there is no evidence that he ever imagined what we call modern democracy. He was not an economist; he probably never dreamed of anything resembling our technological society.

I find in the teachings of Jesus not the slightest suggestion of any ideology at all, nor any sort of political or economic program. I discover no hint of either "Christian economics" or "Christian Marxism." He champions neither socialism nor capitalism, neither democracy nor class rule.

HALF-TRUTHS OR WHOLE GOSPEL?

Let me add here that I see no announcement of a political strategy in Jesus' "first sermon" (Luke 4:16-21). I am familiar with the frequent use that is made of his quotation from Isaiah:

> *The Spirit of the Lord is upon me,*
> *because he has anointed me to preach*
> *good news to the poor.*
> *He has sent me to proclaim release to*
> *the captives*
> *and recovering of sight to the blind,*
> *to set at liberty those who are oppressed,*
> *to proclaim the acceptable year of the*
> *Lord.*

Contrary to some popular interpretations, however, I see no solid basis for politicizing this statement. To read it as if Jesus were presenting a political program—or asking us to—is to do violence to his ministry. These words have to be read in the light of everything else he said and did, which is what we are trying to examine here.

Christ's command is clear: love your neighbor. The implication seems equally clear: build an economy, a political order, a social structure that will enable your fellow citizen to achieve the best possible life.

The implementation? Here we argue and debate and struggle. I for one see Christians on both sides of just about every phase of this conflict. Every practical proposal for the implementation of Christian concern has to be tested not by the New Testament, but by arguments drawn from political science and experience, from economic theory and business practice, from sociological studies and real history.

Who Is My Neighbor?

For instance, some of the parables of Jesus lend themselves to different interpretations, depending on the understanding of politics and economics one brings to them. The simplest illustration of this is the story of the last judgment: "I was hungry, estranged, in prison, and you ministered to me."

How do we minister to our troubled, hurt, estranged, deprived neighbors, for whom God is so gravely concerned? Conventionally this question has been answered in terms of social service. Church groups join in acts of charity: we distribute food to the hungry, collect clothing for the poor, visit those in prison.

But, in our generation, the question is being raised whether social services of this sort are sufficient. It is said that we need social reforms that will get at the conditions which cause people to suffer in these ways. So the argument runs, it is not enough to visit jails; we must reform the prison system. It is not enough to give away food and old clothes; we must organize our economy so that everybody gets a fair share of our affluence. We must free people from their ghettoes, give them education and opportunity for work and housing. What is needed is not social service but social change.

Frankly, I have to say that, to me, the logic is inescapable. It seems perfectly apparent that our political and economic structures help determine how people are treated. Political power can be manipulated in such a way as to deprive citizens of their rights and privileges. Our economic system can operate in such a way that those who are already disadvantaged are deprived of opportunities to live better. Our social customs can effectively block some people from the sort of living conditions they would like to enjoy.

It looks as if the only way to relieve the hurt and discrimination being suffered by many of our people is to change the ways of organizing our common life, to reform the way we handle such things as employment, housing, etc. Change only comes by the application of pressure on those who benefit from the present system. We who have power will not relinquish it, or share it, unless we are forced to do so by some opposing power. (Protestations of love to the contrary notwithstanding, that's the way we are.)

What I have called the logic of this position is not equally apparent to all my fellow Christians. But it seems to me that to deny the need for change and reform is to say that the present systems and structures serve our Christian purposes very well. This is exactly the debate. This is a political and economic judgment just as certainly as is the advocacy of change. To say that Christian purposes can best be implemented through present structures is just as much a politicizing of love as the argument that love requires radical social change.

Both arguments have to meet the test of economic and political theory and experience. Here the New Testament is not our textbook. The disciplines of political science, economics, sociology, and the practical experience of our own history are our sources of instruction.

So as we inquire into what kinds of social change may be called for, we once again find ourselves embroiled in conflict. And I think the churches ought

Who Is My Neighbor?

to be centers of discussion, frequently heated and argumentative. Churches should be centers for study and learning and growth, perhaps even centers for stimulating specific kinds of social action.

Those who lack power seem to be of special concern to God: the man beaten and robbed; those who are hungry, alienated, imprisoned. He calls these— even "the least" of them—"my brethren."

I cannot conclude from this, as some of my colleagues do, that because God is "on the side of the poor and depressed," he is "against the rich and powerful." This is to interpret the gospel by an ideology. (Those are real quotations too.)

As I read the record, God is equally concerned for the good of all men. Remember? He loves our "enemies," maybe even our political and economic opponents. But Jesus does indicate that God identifies especially with people who are suffering indignities and deprivations at the hand of their fellow men. He calls us to a similar concern, and to action which implements that concern.

So let us debate the kinds of action which must be taken, but not stall the action by endless discussion. We may argue the wisdom of policies and programs, but we cannot evade the necessity of taking practical and specific action.

Remember, it is always easy to deceive ourselves at these points. Our self-interest is very powerful, and very tricky. Really to be concerned about the good of others does not come easy. We can hide our lack of love behind our high-sounding arguments.

We need to be open and honest. Loving, maybe?

Half-Truths or Whole Gospel?

THE HEART OF THE MATTER

A host of practical issues are involved in this whole inquiry. I can't begin to address myself to all of them.

For instance, in our day of mass communications we are exposed to a range of need that is literally worldwide. We see on the television screen the actual results of flood and famine on the other side of the world. The total suffering of humanity is immeasurable.

If the teaching of Jesus is to be taken literally, every one of these needy human beings has a claim upon us. But how can we stand this? How can we live under such an intolerable burden?

There are other and immediate needs to which we have to respond. I have a family, and they have first claim on me. There are community needs with which we must concern ourselves. National problems cry out for attention.

In all this welter of claims and demands, how do we respond in a Christian manner?

All I can say is, every person has to arrange the priorities of his own life. Obviously, we cannot respond to every need or give ourselves to every claim. We have to evaluate them and assign priorities. No one else can do this for us. Yet we can work it out in concert—family, church, community organizations, political and economic alliances. As individuals we will surely function in community with others.

But let's never try to reduce the demand which is laid upon us. Here is where it would be easy to fall into the second half-truth that plagues the churches. It seems all too easy to identify the gospel with particular kinds of social change. The divine imperative then becomes a program for specific social action, and the fullness of the gospel is reduced to a half-truth.

The imperative under which we live demands something deeper than action. It demands an attitude, a concern, a commitment to one another in the name of Christ. This requires an inner transformation much deeper than mere activity.

We respond in obedience to a command. God says, Love your neighbor. He makes no exceptions, no adjustments to our limitations. The command is absolute.

God does more than command. He identifies with those who have a claim on our love. He assures us that in loving others we are serving him.

And more: God gives himself to those he loves, to all of us. He comes to us in our hostility and violence. He seeks to cleanse us at the deepest level of our motivation. He gives himself to us, to all men, in the hope that we will allow his love to release us from self-interest, to free us into real caring for one another. He wants us to be his children, to manifest the love he gives us.

"Be merciful, even as your Father is merciful." (Luke 6:36.)

V

What Do YOU Say?

One of the most startling incidents in the life of Jesus is the occasion for the next question. Most of us are familiar with the story in a general sort of way. At least, we know the punch line: "Let him who is without sin," etc.

Interestingly enough, you may have trouble finding the story in your New Testament. In the King James Version, it is familiarly and comfortably where we have learned that it belongs, at the beginning of the eighth chapter of John's Gospel. But if you consult the Revised Standard Version, you will find the story consigned to a footnote at the bottom of the page; and in the New English Bible, as an appendix at the end of the Gospel.

What's the reason for this handling of the account? The answer to the question provides an occasion for a little excursion into a different aspect of New Testament study.

Behind the New Testament, as we know it, lies a bewildering array of documents, the study of which requires the special skills of scholars. There are literally

What Do You Say?

thousands of manuscripts, some of the entire New Testament, some of particular books, some consisting of just bits and pieces. These manuscripts were compiled during the early centuries of the Christian era. Many of the major churches in the cities of the Mediterranean world had their own copies of the documents of the New Testament. They were not always the same books, nor were they necessarily the same in every detail. Some were in Greek. Others, for obvious reasons, were in the half dozen languages used in that part of the world at that time in history.

One whole phase of New Testament scholarship is the patient, careful study and comparison of these many documents. Such scholarly work is seldom apparent to us everyday readers of the Bible, but it goes on all the time. It is the only way to determine just what may be the best "reading" of particular passages. As a consequence of it all, we know we have a New Testament that is entirely dependable.

Now back to the particular story we are considering here. Interestingly enough, this event is not recorded in some of the oldest and best manuscripts of the Fourth Gospel. In others, it is reported at another point in Christ's ministry. The obvious conclusion is that the story does not necessarily belong at the specific point at which we have traditionally found it; but it seems equally clear that it is a genuine account of a real event. What happens here is entirely compatible with the whole ministry of Jesus. This particular event illuminates brilliantly what we all recognize as the authentic character of Jesus.

HALF-TRUTHS OR WHOLE GOSPEL?

THE INCIDENT

Early in the morning he came again to the temple; all the people came to him, and he sat down and taught them. The scribes and the Pharisees brought a woman who had been caught in adultery, and placing her in the midst they said to him, "Teacher, this woman has been caught in the act of adultery. Now in the law Moses commanded us to stone such. What do you say about her?" This they said to test him, that they might have some charge to bring against him. Jesus bent down and wrote with his finger on the ground. And as they continued to ask him, he stood up and said to them, "Let him who is without sin among you be the first to throw a stone at her." And once more he bent down and wrote with his finger on the ground. But when they heard it, they went away, one by one, beginning with the eldest, and Jesus was left alone with the woman standing before him. Jesus looked up and said to her, "Woman, where are they? Has no one condemned you?" She said, "No one, Lord." And Jesus said, "Neither do I condemn you; go, and do not sin again."—John 8:2-11

Jesus was teaching in one of the open spaces of the Temple grounds. He was seated, eastern style, talking quietly with those who were gathered around him.

Suddenly they were rudely interrupted. A knot of men shouldered their way through the group of listeners. The way they were dressed indicated that they were representatives of the religious and scholarly leaders of the nation. (You might say that some wore clerical collars and others wore academic hoods.) Their positions were clearly indicated by their apparel. But there was nothing either pious or learned about the

What Do You Say?

look on their faces. They were strained with anger mixed with lust.

As they pushed into the open space before Jesus, they thrust before him a young woman, weeping, shamefaced, disheveled.

Teacher, they said, we caught this woman in the very act of adultery. According to the circumstances, the law says she should be stoned to death. What do you say?

Jesus refused to answer. He leaned forward and traced on the ground with his finger. He may have been angry at these men, and trying to maintain his composure. He knew they wanted to trick him, and were willing to use this girl—already miserably used—for their purposes.

It was as if Jesus were saying to these self-righteous, devious men: I'm not going to play your game. You are exploiting this girl, trying to get at me. I'll have nothing to do with it.

But the men would not be put off. They pressed their question: You are a self-styled teacher. Well, here's a clear-cut case about which the law gives clear-cut instructions. What is your advice? What do you say?

By this time Jesus had control of himself. Rising to his feet so he could look the accusers in the eye, he replied, "Let him who is without sin among you be the first to throw a stone at her" (v. 7).

It was as if he said, You may do what the law requires. I will not dispute that. But let the execution be started by the one who does not himself deserve some punishment.

Chagrined and embarrassed, the men withdrew. Finally, there were left only Jesus, seated again and quietly tracing figures in the sand, the woman trying to compose herself, and the taut circle of those who had observed the drama from its beginning.

After a little while, Jesus looked up at the woman and said, Well, is there nobody left to carry out the sentence?

She replied, No one.

And Jesus said, Well, I'm not going to act as your executioner either. Just don't let it happen again.

(And I'll bet it didn't!)

THE ATTITUDE OF JESUS

There are three elements in the attitude of Jesus which are characteristic not only of this incident but of his entire ministry.

First, Jesus always displayed a clear, unquestioned integrity. He was a man of such transparent honesty that no one was ever able to prove anything unsavory against him.

His opponents tried. They trumped up charges. Oddly enough, one of the most serious accusations they leveled against Jesus was that he was careless about the company he kept. He was not embarrassed to talk with prostitutes or to visit with businessmen of shady reputation. But no one ever successfully accused him of joining in any shady deals or engaging in any dubious indulgences.

Nothing in this particular event compromises his integrity. He does not condone the woman's error. He does not say that what had happened did not matter.

What Do You Say?

It did matter, desperately. The woman had been badly used, and may herself have consented to the abuse.

Incidentally, let us not jump to the conclusion that this event implies a double standard of sexual morality. As I understand it, the Law considered adultery to be a serious crime for the man too. Only in certain circumstances was special punishment inflicted on the woman. Apparently, this was such a situation.

So the woman was guilty. She knew it. Jesus knew it. He did not minimize her guilt. But he saw that she needed forgiveness more than anything else; and, in his own quiet way, he offered it.

He said, I will not act as your executioner. But please don't let anything like this happen again.

The second mark of Jesus' attitude is his impatience with pride and self-righteousness. In a way, this quality is the other side of his integrity. His very honesty made him reject all pretense. His own sense of dependence upon God enabled him to see the hollowness of self-righteousness.

This is why Jesus was so hard on the Pharisees. They were not such undesirable characters. They were, in fact, very decent people. They followed the teachings of their religion carefully. They were responsible citizens. They tried to do what was right.

The only trouble was that many of them considered that their decency put them in a very special class. They thought themselves better than most people. They were proud of their moral achievements, and they were quite sure that their decency earned them the favor of God. As a consequence, they were indifferent to those who were down and out.

HALF-TRUTHS OR WHOLE GOSPEL?

This is what Jesus had to reject with unsparing honesty. In a striking reversal of popular religion, Jesus was accepting of those who were considered morally disreputable, and he was biting in his criticism of the respectable religious leaders.

Just because, in this particular incident, Jesus did not openly condemn the erring girl, don't conclude that he never spoke judgmentally. If you want to hear how he lashed out at false and pretentious attitudes, just read the twenty-third chapter of Matthew. Here the author seems to have collected many of the hard words that Jesus used in his confrontations with the scribes and Pharisees.

"Woe to you, scribes and Pharisees, hypocrites! . . . You blind men! . . . You are like whitewashed tombs. . . . You serpents, you brood of vipers!"

This is strong language, biting, sure to arouse anger. And this is Jesus, "meek and mild," speaking.

It was his own integrity which wrung from him such anguished attacks upon the one sin he found it so difficult to unmask, self-righteousness. He knew (as Paul did after him) that such an attitude is just as destructive and damning as the more obvious misdeeds which catch the attention and condemnation of most religious and ethical teachers.

The third mark of Jesus' attitude toward others is his profound compassion for those who were exploited and suffered discrimination. These were precisely the ones who were neglected by conventional religion. Jesus deliberately sought them out. He wanted them to know that God really cared about them. He understood his own actions as being expressive of divine love.

What Do You Say?

When Jesus was criticized for keeping company with the moral outcasts, he simply replied, That's the way God is. And that's why I'm here, to demonstrate what God is like.

After all, he said, a doctor does not spend all his time with friends who are enjoying good health; a doctor works with those who are sick. He continued, I have not come to enjoy the company of those who are well, but to bring healing to the sick (Luke 5:29-32, and parallel passages).

Jesus knew perfectly well that the well-to-do, decent citizens were sick, as well as the down-and-outers. Indeed, the scribes and Pharisees may have been even more seriously ill. They did not realize, or would not admit, that they were sick, so they refused to do anything about it. And they rejected Jesus' efforts to disclose and heal their trouble. Precisely because they thought they were good enough, they refused to hear his teaching about the freely offered love of God.

So Jesus turned to those who were open to his approach, those who were being put down and discriminated against by the respectable religious people. These outcasts knew they had no hope from conventional religion, so they responded gladly to Jesus' open, accepting attitude. They were glad to hear that this is really what God is like.

So Jesus was able to say something that is just as shocking today as it was then: People like this who are open to the love of God will enter the Kingdom rather than those who appear to be religiously correct but are complacent and self-righteous (Matthew 21:31*b*-32).

Half-Truths or Whole Gospel?

Jesus was always trying to evoke such openness to God. And his own compassion is seen as the expression of the seeking love of God.

HOW CAN WE BECOME?

All of us know that this is the kind of people we should be. These reflections on the character of Jesus are already familiar to us. There is nothing new here. We've heard this most of our lives. We know, with a kind of dismay, the sort of person Jesus wants us to be.

The real tragedy of the church is that we resemble the Pharisees more than we resemble Jesus. Put us in the main event we are considering in this chapter, and we appear to be standing with the self-righteous people who were abusing the guilty woman, rather than with Jesus in his sensitive openness to her.

The church may not be as bad as it looks, but there is no doubt about its appearance. We give the impression of being pharisaical.

To the extent that we think we are the decent, respectable segment of society, we do indeed resemble the Pharisees.

To the extent that we look with disdain on the alienated and angry, we are in fact pharisaical.

To the extent that we are trusting our own religiousness and morality, we look just like the Pharisees.

The words of Jesus are directed at us. Who are we to throw stones?

How can we be transformed from this sort of person and become what we know he wants us to be? There is no doubt that we want to be followers of Christ.

What Do You Say?

We want to be useful members of his church. We know this means manifesting the kind of openness and sensitivity which Jesus expressed. How can we combine integrity and compassion?

Frankly, I think we must recognize the impossibility of being this kind of persons without God's help. We must admit that the only way we can become truly compassionate persons is to be transformed by the grace of God.

We have to go back to a troubling word of Jesus which we noted earlier. With men this kind of compassion is impossible, but not with God. With God all things are possible, even this.

That is to say, we begin by recognizing that we are sinners. We do not stand in judgment of this girl. We stand with her, under the judgment of God. We need —as desperately as she—to hear the forgiving words of Jesus.

We can then be what our parents used to call "sinners saved by grace." No matter how long we are members of the church, or how faithfully we serve, we are never anything other than "sinners saved by grace." That is, we have been as wayward as the guilty girl, if not in physical act then certainly in unworthy motive. Our only reliance is just what hers became, trust in the compassionate concern of Jesus Christ.

If we can keep this perspective, we shall be delivered from self-righteousness. We stand just where every other human being stands. We are no better than they. Acknowledgment of this keeps us from throwing stones at anybody else.

Hopefully, we have gained some personal integrity.

But we can take no pride in it. We know it is the result of God's working in us.

We learn to be compassionate, because we know that we are sinners, graciously forgiven and gratefully sustained by God. Therefore, the only sin with which we may be impatient is the very one to which we ourselves are liable, pride and self-righteousness.

Maybe, in time, we can become persons who can manifest the attitude of acceptance and speak the word of kindness that Jesus expressed. But it will take some time. That suggests what I believe is the second resource for enabling us to become Christ's kind of person.

THE COUNSELOR

All too often we neglect the fact that the Christian life is a process. We are intended to grow. Being a Christian does not mean we have arrived at a destination. It means we are on the way toward a goal. The Christian life, then, is a process of growing toward the fulfillment we believe God intends for us.

God wants to help us in this development. This is the deepest meaning of the teaching about the Holy Spirit. The process of Christian growth is the work of God's Spirit in us.

We must not expect to find in the teachings of Jesus any complete body of doctrine about the Holy Spirit. Such discovery and development had to wait for the further experiences of Christ's followers. These followers had to experience the mystery of God's presence with them and the miracle of his power in them.

What Do You Say?

Then they were able to speak with some understanding about the Holy Spirit.

According to the Fourth Gospel, Jesus did give some indication to his disciples that they could expect further developments in their religious experience. He had not been able to tell them everything; there was more for them to learn. All was not over just because he was going to leave them; new experiences were waiting for them. And all this would be the work of the Spirit of God.

These teachings are found in the latter chapters of the Fourth Gospel. These extraordinary chapters reflect some of the last things Jesus said to his disciples. The disciples and Jesus were together in the Upper Room on the eve of his death. Jesus talked with them at length, quietly, thoughtfully. He spoke of many things. He left a promise of future resources by which they would be enabled to live well.

> *I will pray the Father, and he will give you another Counselor, to be with you for ever, even the Spirit of Truth, whom the world cannot receive, because it neither sees him nor knows him; you know him, for he dwells with you, and will be in you.—John 14:16-17*

> *These things I have spoken to you, while I am still with you. But the Counselor, the Holy Spirit, whom the Father will send in my name, he will teach you all things, and bring to your remembrance all that I have said to you.—John 14:25-26*

> *When the Counselor comes, whom I shall send to you from the Father, even the Spirit of truth,*

HALF-TRUTHS OR WHOLE GOSPEL?

who proceeds from the Father, he will bear witness to me.—John 15:26

I have yet many things to say to you, but you cannot bear them now. When the Spirit of truth comes, he will guide you into all the truth; for he will not speak on his own authority, but whatever he hears he will speak, and he will declare to you the things that are to come. He will glorify me, for he will take what is mine and declare it to you.—John 16:12-14

We must not be sidetracked into interesting literary and critical issues related to these paragraphs. There are lots of them. Let us try to understand the clear meaning of these words for our lives.

Jesus is promising his disciples—including us, I would think—that after he leaves, they will be given a new and different experience of the presence and power of God. God will be present with them personally, intimately, deeply. He will enable them to become effective followers of Christ.

The Greek word which is used to identify this presence of God is Counselor. It is sometimes translated as "one called alongside to help." We all know what a counselor is. Most of us have needed one at some time or other, a trusted advisor whose guidance we could follow. Jesus is saying that we, his disciples, may experience God with us as Counselor.

Jesus speaks of him as the Spirit of truth. Truth for the author of this Gospel is never abstract and general, but always personal and active. Truth is love in action. God is love in action. His Spirit in us is present as power to enable us to act in loving ways.

WHAT DO YOU SAY?

It is interesting to note that the author suggests that "the world" cannot receive this Spirit. That is, people who don't care about Christ cannot experience the presence and power of God in the same way as those who are his disciples. If we are open to God, he can be present in us, even more deeply than we may realize.

The work of God's Spirit is to stimulate growth in our capacity to show the compassion of Christ. He will teach us what compassion means, what it requires of us. He will guide us into compassionate ways. What is required on our part is our openness to his presence, our honesty in receiving his guidance.

Here is one of the most exciting and promising opportunities ever opened to us. God wants to help us become the kind of person he intends us to be. God can help us grow into the sort of persons we deeply want to be. This is the hope and promise of Christian growth.

THE COMMUNITY OF LOVE

There is a further dimension to the experience of growth, the social dimension. We do not grow in isolation from others but in association with others. We need the support and encouragement of other likeminded people, who are committed to the same kind of life. We need a place to practice the skills we want to develop.

That's what the church is supposed to be, a community of acceptance and support. The church is intended to be an association of people with similar commitments and purposes who accept one another as they are, on the basis of their common convictions. The church is supposed to be a community of people who are supporting one another in common efforts at growth and achievement.

The fact is, as we have repeatedly noted, to love other human beings is frequently—usually—very difficult. We need all the help we can get. We need a place to practice, and that's what the church is supposed to be.

Once again we cannot expect a well-developed doctrine of the church in the teachings of Jesus himself. That had to wait on the later experiences of his followers. It was only after they had lived and worked together as a group of Christians that they took time to reflect on their relationships. Then they developed a more careful statement of what the church really is.

Few specific references to the church are made in Christ's teachings, but there is one statement which I believe is far more significant than is frequently recognized.

You will probably be surprised at the passage I mean, for it is not among those usually referred to in speaking of the church. In fact, the statement is most often quite misinterpreted, at the expense of our life together in the church.

I do not refer to Jesus' words to Peter, "On this rock I will build my church" (Matthew 16:17). Any discussion of this would take us too far afield.

Neither do I refer to the familiar words, "that they may all be one" (John 17:21). For some reason, I have never been deeply impressed with the practical ecumenical significance of this statement. I guess I am

What Do You Say?

more impressed with the ironic fact that from the very beginning there have been tensions and divisions in the Christian church. The first generation of Christ's followers were already quarreling among themselves about what they were supposed to do and to teach. Whatever unity there may have been was marked by serious differences.

The statement of Jesus which seems to me to define his deepest intent for the church is found among his thoughtful musings at the Last Supper. "A new commandment I give to you, that you love one another. By this all men will know that you are my disciples, if you have love for one another." (John 13:34-35; cf. also 15:12.)

Let's look rather carefully at these words. They are addressed to Jesus' disciples. He is not talking to the general public, but to those who have shared his mission. They have taken all the risks involved in following him. They have borne all the costs of their commitment.

He says to his followers: Here is a new commandment. I want you to care about one another as I have cared about you. You are to love one another not just as you love yourselves—that's the way you are to love your neighbors. I want you, my disciples, to love one another as I have loved you, that is, sacrificially. You are to seek one another's good with even greater concern than you seek your own good. This is the way people will know you are my disciples, by the quality of love which you show for one another.

Jesus is not saying to his disciples, I want you to go out and love every Tom, Dick, and Mary. He had said that on other occasions. He had exhorted people to love their neighbors, their fellow human beings.

What he is saying here is: There must be a special quality of love among you who are my followers. In your common commitment to me, you are to care about each other. As a consequence of your common experience of my presence with you, you are enabled to love one another in a special manner.

I believe that Jesus still wants to say this to his followers; but we have managed to misread his words so that we are incapable of receiving their meaning. The church is intended to be a community of people committed to Jesus Christ and capable of caring about one another in a special way that grows out of their experience of his Spirit.

It is obvious that our churches are not such communities. I contend that one reason they are not is because we have lost the true meaning of this particular word of Jesus. We have read it as if he were saying, By this shall all men know that you are my disciples, if you love your neighbor. But he did not say that. He said, The evidence of who you are is the way you love one another as fellow disciples.

Some people will protest that this is too exclusive. But it is exclusive precisely for the sake of enabling us to become inclusive. This command to love our brothers-in-Christ does not displace the command to love our neighbors-in-society. The "new" commandment is given in order to help us to fulfill the second of the two "great" commandments. It is no simple or easy thing to care about—seriously to care about—our fellow human beings. We need a place to practice. We need a community in which are enough common values and aspirations that we can learn to trust and rely on each other.

Let's face it. It isn't easy to trust people we don't know. It's difficult to care about what happens to people who are nameless and faceless. We need to be associated with some people with whom we share enough common commitments that we do trust one another. We need to be part of a group with some common goals, so that we can share—and care about —what happens to one another. The church is supposed to be such a group.

We need a community that will support us in our efforts to become truly compassionate people. We do not always do well. We are frequently rather unlovely persons. We need some people who will stand by us, who will show some compassion toward us. We are strengthened by such association. That's what the church is supposed to offer.

This is not the whole truth about the church. It does not supplant what we have said about the church as servant community, but it is a necessary part of the truth—and a sadly neglected one. We have misplaced this understanding of the church, and our life together suffers as a consequence. The church is little different from our associations in other clubs and organizations, precisely because we don't expect it to be any different, or we don't know how it is supposed to be different.

As a consequence we are robbed of a very important resource for our personal growth and for our life in society. The church as servant community must also be the church as nurturing community. We need to experience growth and development and increasing fulfillment as persons who really care about our fellow human beings. The church is meant to be a community which nurtures such growth. Moreover, we need to be able to express this growing concern for our neighbors in practical ways. The church is intended to be a community of persons working together, supporting and strengthening one another in our lives of Christian love.

Service without nurture becomes forced and anxious and unproductive. Nurture without service becomes self-seeking, self-centered, self-righteous. What we do must express what we are. What we are must issue in what we do. The church exists to help us be and do. Nurture and service constitute the wholeness of our Christian life together.

Why not try to recapture Christ's whole intention? Let us open ourselves to his love and power in such a way that our associations in his church will take on a new quality. Let us see one another as honest and sincere followers of Christ. Let us trust one another. Let us stand by one another.

As a matter of practical fact, our churches as presently constituted probably cannot become such communities. We must form smaller groups within our congregations, in which we will come to common trust and support. So our churches will become clusters of churches. That is, our larger congregations will have within them many kinds of smaller groupings.

Most of our traditional and conventional associations in the church will not be adequate for this purpose. They are already riddled with tensions and

What Do You Say?

hostilities and rivalries. We have to find new ways of relating to one another, new groupings, new purposes for being together.

In this way we will grow in our capacity for integrity and compassion. We can strengthen one another in moral courage. We can encourage one another in compassionate concern.

People will know whose disciples we are, if we really care about one another.

VI
What Is Truth?

One of the most dramatic confrontations in history is the setting for a final and searching question. A middle-grade Roman administrator was caught in a situation he did not quite know how to handle. Before him stood a Jewish prisoner whose quiet self-possession was unnerving.

A strange irony exists in one aspect of the events leading up to this confrontation. (See John 18:28-32.)

Jesus' accusers were bringing him to Pilate on trumped-up charges, and they knew it. They were intent on only one thing, not a fair trail, but the conviction of the prisoner. They were determined to get rid of him.

When they came to the palace where Pilate was staying, however, they refused to enter. Their religious scruples prohibited their entering an "unclean" place so near the time for a religious feast. In order to be clean enough to observe the feast, they refused to go into the Roman palace. So Pilate had to come out to them.

What Is Truth?

The awful irony is this: They were bent on an act of gross injustice, but they were very careful about ritualistic niceties. Their religion told them to be careful where they went. But they ignored its teachings about justice and honesty.

It is true that they considered the prisoner dangerous. He was a subversive, a revolutionary. They had to get rid of him in order to maintain law and order; but they were quite willing to abuse law and order so as to achieve what they considered to be desirable ends. That is dangerous business, both then and now.

Those of us who are concerned about law and order ought to be sensitive to the fact that we can abuse the very structures of law and order in accomplishing ends which we think are good. We ought to be alert to this temptation. Our religious faith ought to keep us sensitive to the demand for justice, even mercy.

THE INCIDENT

The only charge that Jesus' accusers could put together was essentially religious. This was part of Pilate's problem. The prisoner was accused of teaching subversive ideas, but they were religiously subversive. And the Roman official had no equipment for dealing with that.

The Roman genius, like the American, was in politics and technology. They knew how to organize an Empire, and keep it running. But they had little gift for religion, in which they were imitative, eclectic.

So Pilate was not sure he had any jurisdiction over this particular case. He probably sensed trouble and wanted to avoid it. But he heard the testimony, and then called in the prisoner.

> *Pilate entered the praetorium again and called Jesus, and said to him, "Are you the King of the Jews?" Jesus answered, "Do you say this of your own accord, or did others say it to you about me?" Pilate answered, "Am I a Jew? Your own nation and the chief priests have handed you over to me; what have you done?" Jesus answered, "My kingship is not of this world; if my kingship were of this world, my servants would fight, that I might not be handed over to the Jews; but my kingship is not from the world." Pilate said to him, "So you are a king?" Jesus answered, "You say that I am a king. For this I was born, and for this I have come into the world, to bear witness to the truth. Every one who is of the truth hears my voice." Pilate said to him, "What is truth?"—John 18:33-38*

Pilate put out a test question: Are you really the King of the Jews?

The prisoner replied (I hardly know in what spirit), Did you come to this conclusion by yourself? Or did somebody tell you?

Now that really was no way to talk to a Roman official. Pilate was understandably annoyed. So he said rather curtly, Look, I'm no Jew. It's your own people who have brought you here. Why? What have you done?

Jesus, returning to the first question, replied, I have a kingdom which is not at all like Rome or any of the earthly powers you know about. My kingdom is not to be defended by arms and political power.

Then you are a king? Pilate responded, still asking.

WHAT IS TRUTH?

Jesus answered, Yes, that's right. King may be the best word. This is really the reason I am here, to bear witness to the truth.

Then Pilate's timeless question: What is truth?

WILLINGNESS TO FACE IT

I have often wondered what Pilate's attitude was when he asked that question. I really feel sorry for him. He was being backed against a wall by forces and events which he could neither avoid nor control. He knew that a tough moral demand was being forced on him. He was afraid of it.

His question, then, was a troubled attempt to evade the issue. Even as he asked it, he knew it was a dodge, because he knew the answer to his own question.

The answer was standing right in front of him. A quiet man, obviously innocent but utterly fearless, embodied the truth that Pilate was afraid to face. The Roman ruler knew what he should do but he did not have the courage. Even as he muttered the question, he must have known he would never be given the answer —for lack of courage.

The truth for Pilate at that moment was to acknowledge the integrity of Jesus. He could not do it. So he would never really know the truth. Neither will we, if we are afraid, and hesitant, and dishonest.

Knowledge of truth requires courage even more than intellect, because truth is profoundly personal. The question about truth is not primarily technological or logical. It is first of all moral and personal.

Truth confronts us as Jesus Christ, requiring our response, seeking our commitment. He is most likely to confront us precisely at a moment of decision and demand.

This is an understanding of reality which Christian faith tries to maintain but which always slips out of our grasp. It is easier to reduce truth to a dogma to be believed or a rule to be followed or an institution to be supported. But when we do this, we have something less than the true insight of the gospel.

Truth is not a logical proposition but a loving person. Truth is not an abstract idea, but a living being. Truth is not a dogma about Jesus, but Christ himself.

Knowledge of the truth, then, is not intellectual assent but an act of courage. To know the truth is a matter not of mastering information, but of being mastered by a Lord. To speak the truth is not to recite a creed but to live in obedience. To be truthful is not to perform a series of prescribed deeds but to be faithful to Jesus Christ.

Jesus himself is the answer to Pilate's question, and ours.

TRUTH AS PERSON

Unknown to Pilate, but known to us, Jesus had spent the previous evening with his disciples. After a rather somber supper, they remained at the table, and Jesus talked with them quietly. (Cf. John's Gospel, chapters 13–17.)

It is as if I were a vine, he said, and you the branches. You must be deeply committed to me, so that you may experience love, joy, peace (chap. 15).

You are going to run into trouble. The world will

What Is Truth?

actually hate you, as it has me. But keep up your spirits. I have overcome all these troubles (chap. 16).

Don't be anxious in all this. Trust God. Trust me, and I will be with you more deeply and truly than you can quite imagine (chap. 14. [The reordering of these chapters is after a suggestion by James Moffatt, a great British New Testament scholar]).

The followers of this man have found these words confirmed in their own experience. They have concluded, and we with them, that this man is indeed the truth, a truth we can know deeply, personally.

Truth is Person. We know the truth when we open ourselves to this Person.

TRUTH AS AGONY

Unknown to Pilate, but known to us, Jesus had spent part of the preceding night in lonely agony. Facing an ugly death, he was repulsed. But he realized that this was part of a larger enterprise in which he was involved. So he was able at last to say, All right, I'll do what you want me to do.

His followers have learned that the deepest kind of truth is not learned in cool detachment, but in agony and uncertainty. Truth is trust wrung from terror.

TRUTH AS CARING LOVE

Pilate could not know, as we do, what would happen as a result of his faltering decision. This prisoner would be stretched between heaven and earth in a posture of disgrace and rejection. Yet his followers would come to worship this very form.

Truth is cruciform. Truth is love with arms outstretched to embrace suffering, so as to heal those who suffer.

TRUTH AS POWER

Pilate could not know, as we do, that just a few days after the death of this strange prisoner a whole new dimension of reality would be opened to humanity.

On the third day after Jesus' death, a rumor began to be whispered through the streets of the capital. This man is not dead. Death could not hold him. God has raised him up!

The strange rumor became a great shout of faith. And the Christian gospel became the most astounding affirmation the world has ever known.

God affirms his power of life over death. God has conquered death and all that death stands for, defeat and absurdity. All the death-dealing forces that spoil our lives are defeated. We need not live in fear and anxiety and distrust. We can trust ourselves to the God who shares his power of life.

Truth is life-giving power. To open ourselves to this truth is to experience a new quality of effectiveness and fulfillment.

CONCLUSION

So we have circled back to our first question. But it is not a simple recall. We return to the first question with a deeper understanding of its answer.

To whom shall we go? To Jesus Christ. For he is the truth.

Christ is truth as Person. He shows us that God knows us and cares about us. Indeed, God cares so

What Is Truth?

truly that he gives himself to us in costly love. God's love is suffering love.

Christ's act of love on the cross is the manifestation in history of what is always true in the life of God. If it is possible for us to say that God is love, it is because of what God has done in Jesus Christ. (Cf. I John 4:8-9.)

No wonder the cross has become the central symbol of our faith. It is the sign of the truth that God really cares about us.

The God who cares is the God who conquers. The God whose purpose is love has power to fulfill his purpose. The Crucifixion affirms his caring. The Resurrection is his act of conquering.

The power of life over death is a present power, available to us right now. The power by which Jesus was raised from the dead is the same power by which we may be released from fear and guilt and despair. We have only to grasp this truth, to let Christ take hold of us. And he will give us power to live well.

So the conclusion is a beginning, the beginning of a new life.

Such an understanding and experience of Christian truth will certainly carry us beyond the politics of the present moment in the life of the church. There is a wholeness about the gospel that will dispel the half-truths to which we are tempted to give our allegiance.

But if we are carried beyond politics, we are also returned to politics, with a difference. Commitment to the whole gospel does not, by any means, exempt us from the hard practicalities of policy-making and program-forming in the church. Rather we are given a larger context in which to conduct, and by which to evaluate, our political activities.

So let us return to the continuing political issues that mark the life of the church and of society. We have a common understanding of the complex tasks of the church as servant and nurturing community. Now let us struggle to find ways to implement these tasks. We have a common commitment to Jesus Christ, which enables us to respect one another no matter how earnestly we disagree. We know where our basic loyalty is, and what our shared concerns are. We will not test one another's integrity by whether we agree in all particulars. We are bound together into a body, the head of which is Christ.

Such a hopeful view is based on the assumption that these pages have set forth a reasonable interpretation of the teachings of Jesus. If this is in fact true, I believe we have a basis for a genuine renewal of the church.

If we can honestly agree that the Christian Gospel is approximately what has been set forth in these studies of Christ's teachings, then we can have a common commitment that will hold us together. I cannot think of any political differences that are serious enough to disrupt such unity in Christ. If we are agreed at the point of these basic truths, we can disagree at any number of other points.

Can we manage to open ourselves to the sort of truth which comes to us in Christ? That is really the key question. There are many hindrances in the way.

What Is Truth?

Our continuing study together should help expose and eliminate these. Let us experience the truth which Christ is. He will enable us to become the kind of people who can trust each other, support each other, and work together for the concerns which he lays upon us.